Wrestling the Word

The Hebrew Scriptures and the Christian Believer

Carolyn J. Sharp

First edition
Published by Westminster John Knox Press
Louisville, Kentucky

10 11 12 13 14 15 16 17 18 19—10 9 8 7 6 5 4 3 2 1

Book design by Sharon Adams
Cover design by Eric Walljasper

Library of Congress Cataloging-in-Publication Data

Sharp, Carolyn J.
Wrestling the word : the Hebrew scriptures and the Christian believer / Carolyn J. Sharp.
p. cm.
Includes bibliographical references and index.
ISBN 978-0-664-23067-8 (alk. paper)
1. Bible. O.T.—Introductions. I. Title.
BS1140.3.S43 2010
221.6'1—dc22

2010017889

PRINTED IN THE UNITED STATES OF AMERICA

♾ The paper used in this publication meets the minimum requirements
of the American National Standard for Information Sciences—Permanence
of Paper for Printed Library Materials, ANSI Z39.48-1992.

Westminster John Knox Press advocates the responsible use of our natural resources.
The text paper of this book is made from 30% postconsumer waste.

Wrestling the Word

Also by Carolyn J. Sharp

Old Testament Prophets for Today

For Mom and Mac

Contents

Acknowledgments ix

Introduction xi
- Wrestling the Word xiv
- Diverse Experiences and Goals of Reading xv
- Rereading the Story of Jael and Sisera xvi

1. What's at Stake in Different Ways of Reading 1
- How and Why Do We Read? 2
- Every Interpretation Is Shaped by Context 4
- Arguing over the Author and History 6
- Prior Assumptions and Intuitions 10
- The Role of Tradition 12
- Historical Inquiry 17
- Literary Criticism 22
- Reconfiguring Our Notions of History, Text, and Author 29
- Julia Kristeva: Intertextuality and Foreignness 31
- Emmanuel Lévinas: The Face of the Other and the Interruption of Discourse 37

2. One Truth or Many Voices? Literary Sources and the Integrity of the Text 45
- The Yahwist Doesn't Have Many Friends on Facebook 46
- Why Source Criticism? 48
- Weaknesses of the Method 50
- Around and Around We Go 52
- The Elohist's Last Dance 56

Thinking Anew about Multiple Sources 58
Honoring Diverse Witnesses 59
Gratitude for Fruitful Tensions 60
The Ethics of Attending to Different Voices 63
Walter Brueggemann: Testimony and Countertestimony 64
Mikhail Bakhtin: Dialogical Reading 68

3. Foundational Narratives, History, and Voices from the Margins 77
Bias in Representation 79
The Mystery of Biblical History 81
Influences from Other Ancient Near Eastern Cultures 84
The Potential of Incarnational Theology 88
Diverse Cultural Expressions as Divine Gift 89
Debates about the Historicity of Exodus and Conquest Traditions 90
Dimensions of Truth 96
Redeemed for Obedience 97
Conflicting Assessments of David 100
History with Jael and Sisera 104

4. Insiders and Outsiders: Boundaries and the Theological Imagination 109
Acknowledging Our Situatedness 111
Liberation and Politics 113
Troubling Scripture Texts 115
Feminist and Womanist Readings 116
African and African American Biblical Hermeneutics 122
Queer Readings 124
Postcolonial Criticism 126
Jael and Sisera: Transgendered and Colonized 129

5. Wrestling the Word 135
Collaborative Diaspora Theology 135
Constructing and Reconstructing Your Own Reading Strategies 138

Bibliography 141

Scripture Index 149

Subject Index 151

Acknowledgments

I am grateful for the cheerful and steadfast support of Harold W. Attridge, Henry L. Slack Dean of Yale Divinity School and Lillian Claus Professor of New Testament, in this and all of my scholarly endeavors. A grant from the Griswold Fund of the Whitney Humanities Center at Yale provided important research support at an early stage of this project. I am glad for the lively intellectual stimulation offered by my colleagues, Robert R. Wilson, John J. Collins, and Joel S. Baden, and for the faculty development support graciously provided by Emilie M. Townes, our academic dean and Andrew W. Mellon Professor of African American Religion and Theology.

I am thankful for the Wabash Center for Teaching and Learning in Theology and Religion, which funded a group of scholars to engage in sustained conversation in 2006–2007 about the teaching of biblical exegesis. Members of that consultation remain among my most valued dialogue partners concerning challenges and new horizons in the teaching of biblical interpretation in theological schools. Those colleagues include Margaret Aymer, Greg Carey, Clayton Croy, Jae Won Lee, Esther Menn, Anathea Portier-Young, Andreas Schuele, Matthew Skinner, Brent Strawn, and Christine Roy Yoder.

A final member of that Wabash-funded group deserves special mention. I am blessed to have had a partner toiling in the New Testament side of this particular vineyard: Jaime Clark-Soles, Associate Professor of New Testament at Perkins School of Theology. Jaime has been a cherished friend for almost twenty years, ever since we first met as MDiv students in an intermediate Greek class taught by Walter Wilson. Jaime is an extraordinarily dedicated teacher, a Baptist minister alive with passion for Christ, a wonderful scholar, and the most loyal of friends. It is a joy to know that her book *Engaging the*

Word: The New Testament and the Christian Believer is yoked with this volume of mine on the Hebrew Scriptures.

I am grateful for the gentle guidance and patience of Jon L. Berquist, my editor at Westminster John Knox Press. Jon has been waiting for this book for longer than I'd care to admit, and he has offered just the right blend of kindness, interest, and exhortation along the way. Without his support, this book would not have come into being.

I am humbled by the enduring love and encouragement of my family—especially my husband, Leo; our daughter, Dinah; and our son, Jacob. This book is dedicated to my mother, Sarah D. McAlpin, and my stepfather, the Rev. David H. McAlpin. They have been a constant source of love and support. Their quiet dedication to God and to the life of the church continues to inspire me daily.

Introduction

This book is offered to readers who grapple with unsettling ideas they may have heard about the Hebrew Scriptures in the halls of their church, in the cafeteria of their seminary, or in the public square. Such troubling ideas may include these: that the proliferation of ways of reading the Bible is a sign of degeneration into godless relativism; that the exodus "didn't really happen"; that the Old Testament is hopelessly patriarchal and degrading to contemporary women; and that Israelite ritual observance was legalistic and cannot be illuminating for Christian belief and praxis. The issues lying behind such positions are not just arcane matters about which biblical scholars argue. They matter deeply for theology and for the faith of those who cherish the whole Christian Bible.

In these pages, you will find assessments of some of the lively issues being debated in the guild of biblical scholarship. This book is designed to serve as an introductory guide for seminarians who need help in assessing the theological implications of a daunting array of scholarly arguments in their Old Testament classes. The book is also designed to engage those in the church who no longer read the Hebrew Scriptures seriously because they perceive that part of the Bible to be culturally irrelevant, morally dubious, or alien to their own religious sensibility. I have written this book for clergy and lay believers, for seminarians, and for those who think the Old Testament may be largely irrelevant today. The idea for this project was generated out of my profound appreciation for the struggles and insights of my students. In my ten years of teaching, I have learned much from the wonderfully diverse group of folks from many faith traditions who have studied or are currently studying at Yale Divinity School. They are laypeople, on the path to ordination, or already ordained; they are passionate about Scripture but worried, to one degree or another, about the ethics of the Old Testament; they might claim anything from ardent devotion to "interest in the Old Testament as story" to mild supersessionism to fierce Marcionism in their evaluation of the theological truth of the Hebrew Scriptures; and depending on the day and the topic, they might be convinced that the Old Testament is essential for the life of the church, or they might be convinced that the Old Testament is outdated and has little to say to the contemporary Christian. This book is for them all. I warmly welcome readers of non-Christian heritage or conviction as well, while owning that the purpose of the book is to engage the Hebrew Scriptures in service of Christian theological reflection.

I hope that the hermeneutical and exegetical discussions here will be helpful to first-year seminary and divinity school students who are eager to learn about the Hebrew Scriptures. I want to think with them about what is at stake in particular debates and methods of interpretation. And I want to encourage them as they struggle and soar toward adept, graceful, courageous readings of the biblical text. We professors of biblical studies know well that the introductory Bible course can be challenging for students. Not only is there a vast amount of material to cover. Students also are exposed to new ways of reading, which can be threatening to those who understand faithfulness to Scripture to mean one particular devotional kind of engagement with the Bible. And more: students learn about all kinds of interpretive issues that are seldom mentioned in church. It can be overwhelming and alarming to study the Hebrew Scriptures in a theological school. All learning invites us not only to honor what we already know but also to move beyond that—to journey into new realms of wisdom and new ways of thinking. Learning can be particularly challenging whenever the topic is something near and dear to our hearts, as is the case for many Christian students of the Bible. Thus, the introductory Old Testament course can present unique and dramatic challenges for students of faith. I dearly hope that this book will assist students in navigating those challenges.

The introductory Bible course—a lecture course in many theological schools, often accompanied by a weekly discussion section—usually has a daunting list of objectives:

- to broaden and deepen students' knowledge of the content of the Bible
- to teach about the historical contexts in which biblical texts were shaped, helping students to understand how social, political, and religious norms in those contexts may have shaped the biblical material
- to require students to acquire knowledge about and skill in a wide variety of hermeneutical methods with diverse aims
- to equip students to reflect on how and what exegesis means

- to invite students to construct a well-educated and integrative approach to biblically based faith

At Yale Divinity School, we are blessed to have an entire year for the introductory Old Testament course and an entire year for the equivalent New Testament course. But in many theological schools, professors are allowed only one semester for each Testament. There is never enough time for adequate teaching about integration of historical, hermeneutical, and theological concerns, even if the professor tries to model such integration from the lectern and even if discussion sections are designed to deal with those questions. Hence this book is intended to facilitate the integrative learning of first-year master's students who may be encountering critical engagement with the Hebrew Scriptures for the first time and who need guidance in assessing the theological implications of the debates that currently enliven scholarship on the Hebrew Scriptures.

I hope this volume will be helpful also for those who teach introductory courses on the Hebrew Scriptures in Christian theological schools. It is designed to frame some discussions for which there is just not enough time in the classroom. Chapter 1 offers reflections on the diverse ways of reading that students may encounter when they engage biblical scholarship in the classroom. Chapter 2 provides a way into theological reflection on the Documentary Hypothesis and related issues of multivocality in Scripture. Chapter 3 probes problems of historicity and scriptural meaning. Chapter 4 introduces students to feminist, African American, queer, and postcolonial understandings of gender, race, sexual identity, and class. Chapter 5 offers some integrative conclusions and invites students to be intentional about constructing their own reading strategies.

The book is intended as a resource for students who want to reflect on the intersections of historical, hermeneutical, and theological concerns in a way that honors both their agency as readers and their faith convictions. It is certainly not intended as a comprehensive textbook on hermeneutical methods, the Documentary Hypothesis, ancient Israelite history, feminist biblical interpretation, or the oeuvres of theologians and philosophers whose ideas I engage (Julia Kristeva, Emmanuel Lévinas, Walter Brueggemann, and Mikhail M. Bakhtin). There are many excellent books that can meet those learning goals. As regards Kristeva, Lévinas, Bakhtin, and Brueggemann, there is no substitute for diving into their wonderfully thought-provoking writings and engaging them firsthand. Rather than aiming at comprehensive treatment, this book has been designed to provide a theologically sensitive map to some of the issues that can trouble Christian believers when they engage in critical study of the Hebrew Scriptures.

WRESTLING THE WORD

The chief metaphor governing this book is the idea of wrestling with Scripture. It is drawn from the story of Jacob wrestling with a divine presence at the Jabbok River (Gen. 32:22–32), a narrative that has richly funded many centuries of Jewish and Christian reflection on the nature of God, the risks of relationship, and the identity of the believing community. For me, the metaphor of wrestling evokes a vigorous, lively engagement that sometimes feels like struggle and sometimes feels like play. God's Word becomes incarnated in the lives of believers through our circling around it and taking hold of it, allowing it to "throw us to the mat," pushing back to discover its power and our own strength in particular circumstances, learning about our vulnerabilities as we try out different "holds" on this ungraspable holy Word.

I invite you to delight in the complexity of the issues addressed here. I have heard it said that an introductory-level text should present things simply so that the novice can understand. But even the novice understands intuitively when a story or poem is complex! Even the first-time reader of Scripture can see how beautifully rich and poignant are these texts, not in spite of but precisely because of their complications. Biblical narratives, poetry, laws, and aphorisms already present us with multiple ways of engaging our minds, hearts, and imaginations. What novices need is not a simplistic presentation of Old Testament themes, a bland summary of key motifs, or the suggestion that a few central ideas can account for all of what ancient Israel is trying to say about God and its own life. No, what novices need is an invitation into the complex dynamics at play in profoundly layered sacred texts such as the Hebrew Scriptures.

The Hebrew Scriptures are characterized by dynamic interactions among many traditions from different time periods and cultural settings in ancient Israelite history. To ignore that complexity, even in an introductory approach, would be drastically to misrepresent the character of the biblical witness. Perhaps worse, it would do a grave disservice to the reader. We know that life is complex and challenging. It is a blessing that our sacred texts in the Bible are complex and challenging too! Otherwise, we could just read Hallmark cards and advertising slogans in church on Sunday mornings ("Love means never having to say you're sorry," or "Because you're worth it," or "Just do it!"). Navigating the complexity of biblical truths in faith is the joy of every believer and the special obligation of everyone training for leadership in the church. I hope this book helps to equip you for that navigation in faith.

DIVERSE EXPERIENCES AND GOALS OF READING

Reading Scripture is like encountering the ocean. As you know, there are many ways to encounter the ocean. You might walk in the pounding surf, allowing the spray of the ocean to dampen your clothes as you ponder some mystery unrelated to the saltwater surging at your knees. Or you might devote your life to a scientific discipline such as marine biology and undergo years of training to gain insight into the phenomena you study. Or you might give your spare time to deep-sea fishing, an arduous sport that requires significant training and expertise. As with marine biology and deep-sea fishing, professional training in the study of Scripture can bring up odd-looking creatures from the depths that no one knows quite what to do with, but which are absolutely fascinating to those who have spotted them. Casual or touristic engagement with the ocean is also possible: you might ride through the ocean in a chartered glass-bottomed boat, hoping to see an eel below the boat or a whale breaching the surface; you might not fully understand what you are seeing, but you will still enjoy it, just as may happen for those readers who encounter the Bible as a source of enrichment in art or film, or who occasionally dip into Scripture without much seriousness of purpose. You can stay close to the surface of a rich variety of texts, as one does when snorkeling to admire the stunning beauty and variety of life around coral reefs. Or you can dive deeper, as deep-sea explorers do who seek out bioluminescent creatures in mile-deep ocean trenches. Historians and literary critics are readers who dive deep to appreciate the beauty, artistry, and strangeness of what God has wrought in Scripture.

You can also float peacefully and tranquilly on the sea: just so, the spiritually oriented reader who seeks comfort in familiar stories or meaningful verses of the Psalms is engaging Scripture in a valuable way that has sustained believers and communities for many centuries. On the other hand, scholars and others preparing to wrestle in a sustained way with Scripture are like those who go into the ocean for long training swims—to strengthen their muscles, improve their endurance, and perfect their form. You may be eager for an invigorating, demanding workout of the inquiring heart and mind that God gave you. All of this is possible, just as there are countless ways to engage the ocean. There is not only one faithful way to read.

A final note: just as you should not swim alone in the ocean because of dangerous and unpredictable currents, so too you should not swim alone in Scripture for too long. Reading can be liberating and powerful and illuminating and intoxicating, but it can also be risky. We can misunderstand; we can get anxious about what we don't understand and then overcompensate by insisting that others must read as we do. The church and the synagogue have always read the Bible in community, for good reason. Communities of readers balance each other and broaden each other's perspectives. We challenge and affirm and nuance our insights in conversation. We test our intuitions against readings that our communities of faith have cherished for centuries. All are the richer for such dialogical engagement.

REREADING THE STORY OF JAEL AND SISERA

As each chapter of this book unfolds, we will reread a biblical tradition that is retailed in two different versions in Scripture: the story of Jael and Sisera, which is found in a prose version in Judges 4 and a poetic rendering in Judges 5. This story will serve as the exegetical "site" at which we will camp as we examine various methodological and theological issues. It is my hope that it will be both informative and enjoyable for you to consider multiple hermeneutical approaches to the tradition of Jael and Sisera as a way of discerning what is at stake in the actual reading of biblical texts according to the cues of various scholarly positions. I encourage you to read Judges 4–5 attentively before consulting the chapters that follow in this book. Indeed, your perspective on aspects of biblical interpretation may change—may deepen, may fracture, may become richer or more complicated—and you may want to reread Judges 4–5 anew with each chapter of this book.

My reasons for choosing the story of Jael and Sisera as a particular place of engagement are two. First, the graphic violence that we see in significant streams of Hebrew Bible tradition constitutes a stumbling block to the appropriation of the theology of the Hebrew Scriptures by many Christian readers. If a violent story such as this can be engaged productively, then readers who have been inclined to dismiss the Old Testament because of its violent rhetoric and stories of war might look at difficult biblical texts with renewed interest. Second, the dearth of women as agents and bearers of tradition within the Hebrew Scriptures has put off some women—and not only those who name themselves feminists—from seeking to understand the potentially rich ways in which the Hebrew Scriptures can invite them into reflection on their own spiritual journeys. In the story of Jael and Sisera, we see a woman who exercises power in a moment of crisis and is commended for it. Women who may have thought only of Sarah and Ruth may now add a lesser-known figure to their storehouse of women characters in the Bible who can help them imagine their own agency as believers.

When we read Scripture, we never read alone. Christian believers encounter these texts in community. You read in the communal context of your own worship tradition as that may have shaped your beliefs, hermeneutics, and spiritual practices over time. If you are a seminary or divinity school student or professor, you also read in the context of your classroom learning community and the larger curriculum, traditions, and fellowship of your theological school. And each of us reads surrounded by those who have gone before: the ancient authors of the Hebrew Scriptures themselves, the New Testament writers who heard these sacred texts with such profound devotion, saints and skeptics, preachers and teachers, dissidents and activists, political leaders and cloistered religious, clergy and scholars, and the countless other believers of many centuries who have wrestled with and found truth in the Hebrew Scriptures. Most importantly, we read in the presence of the One who calls us continually to renewed relationship with the Holy and with one another.

1

What's at Stake in Different Ways of Reading

"Why should I care about the names of the five Philistine city-states? Why on earth do I need to know that?" The first-year MDiv student, a woman in her mid-thirties, was visibly frustrated. I was a teaching assistant in the big Old Testament lecture course at Yale Divinity School. We were reading Amos's oracle against Philistia, and I had probed to see whether anyone in the group could identify the cities in the Philistine pentapolis: Ashkelon, Gath, Ashdod, Gaza, and Ekron. The hostility behind this student's question caught me off guard, and I blushed. I was brand new to teaching, and it had not occurred to me that students might not be eager to master as much knowledge about the subject matter of the Old Testament as they could, the better to interpret these marvelous texts. "Well," I fumbled, "it matters for knowing what some of the prophets are talking about in their oracles against particular nations . . . and, uh . . . for understanding cultural subtexts and . . . uh . . . well, history just matters! If you care about the ancient world in which these texts were written, then you need to know about the history that these texts are reflecting." Compelling answer? Maybe not. But this interchange brought home to me the fact that not only the meaning(s) but even the importance of historically informed reading itself can be contested. Why and how history matters cannot be taken for granted.

But knowing details of historical context cannot alone shed anywhere near adequate light on a text. As a student, I had the experience on numerous occasions of historically minded professors sharing information about the historical context of a biblical text and then ending class—as if we had adequately interpreted a poetic oracle or a narrative simply by naming potential historical factors in its composition! That way of working with history in the act of interpretation is superficial. It ignores poetic artistry, says nothing about the function of characterization and dramatic tension in a story, fails to inquire into the complex cultural associations that are evoked by metaphor, misses the subtle persuasive power of irony, and usually doesn't address the fascinating question of the construction of implied audiences. Simplistic historicizing reading overlooks many crucial dimensions of the biblical text. And it can be terribly boring—except, perhaps, for those who are more interested in the history of ancient Israel than in the text as text.

HOW AND WHY DO WE READ?

What do we privilege when we encounter a biblical text? How do we choose to read? To address that question, we need to explore *why* we read. The act of reading brings us into a place of imaginative encounter with voices, ideas, and languages that are fascinating and foreign to our experience. Through reading, we learn about perspectives that may affirm, challenge, or complicate our understandings of ourselves and others, God, the world, and history. Through reading, we learn new ways to articulate what may be meaningful in our experiences of local and broader human culture. Thus reading is not merely a means to acquire information. Reading is potentially transformative for readers and for reading communities—for my Episcopal parish in New Haven and a Quaker meeting in Sacramento, for a young boy in an elementary school classroom on the south side of Chicago and a middle-aged woman in a feminist book group in Berlin. Reading is powerful—and not only for good. We sometimes encounter ideas that destabilize values or understandings we cherish. We are sometimes convinced too quickly by erroneous, incomplete, or naive views. We are sometimes confronted by lies or hate-filled rhetoric masquerading as truth.

Because reading changes us in powerful ways, we need to attend carefully to the ways in which we read. And when reading Scripture, we need to honor what is at stake for different readers and reading communities when they promote certain kinds of readings over others. Interpreting is always an act of power, and reading sacred texts in communities has consequences. The power of interpretation can be wielded and experienced in ways that are nurturing and illuminating, but it can also mislead, unduly constrain, and deform the understanding.

Passionate disputes over ways to read have divided the church since its earliest days. Lively—and sometimes venomous—disputes still divide the academy when scholars argue about how texts mean, which reading strategies are the most important or most persuasive, and conversely, which hermeneutical assumptions are poorly thought through. These disputes are not just arcane discussions involving scholars slinging arrows at each other from their respective ivory towers. They are deeply relevant to daily life, as anyone will acknowledge who sees the ways in which arguments about reading Scripture play out in church politics and in the public square.

One bitter dispute in the academy has to do with whether and why it is valuable to seek to understand what an author meant when she or he wrote. For historical critics, it goes without saying that authors produce texts with certain purposes in mind and, further, that it is a meaningful activity to try to understand what authors' intentions might have been. But others, particularly in literary circles, have for decades argued strenuously that we can never truly know what an author intended and that it is misguided to try to do so. The intentions of the author are lost to us, as indeed, the intentions may even have been lost to the author herself or himself—for it is not uncommon for a poet or novelist to say, "Well, I don't know exactly what I meant by that line. What does it mean to *you*?" Many literary critics insist that even if authorial intention were somehow recoverable, it should not control the meaning of the text in any definitive way, not even as a starting point for further-ranging creative discussions of meaning.

I remember a dinner at which I debated with someone about the book of Ecclesiastes (the speaker in that text is called Qohelet in the Hebrew). I was interested in arguing for irony in the text, which in my theoretical framework has to imply an ironist, one who intends to mislead. I have always been willing to concede that authorial intention is tricky to discern and may only ever be partially and imperfectly known. I also concede that the ways in which we reconstruct authorial intention are always shaped by our own predispositions and assumptions. But texts were produced by real people whose voices, expressed through the choice of rhetorical strategies and artistic decisions within their texts, should be listened to in any responsible ethic of reading. Their voices are not entirely identical to what we reconstruct in our own image. At the dinner my interlocutor became increasingly aggressive when I would not give up the idea that it matters what the original author was trying to do. "There was no 'Qohelet,'" he insisted, his voice rising. He and others of similar hermeneutical convictions claim forcefully that "texts don't *do* anything," that meaning is produced entirely by the activity of the reader. I agree that we can never encounter a text entirely apart from our own cultural and personal biases. But I disagree with the position that it is fruitless or misguided to try to attend to those ancient voices and visions that have produced texts or other art. Each text provides its own kind of witness whether I understand it or not—indeed, whether I bother to read it or not.

EVERY INTERPRETATION IS SHAPED BY CONTEXT

Take the example of a bird's song. When we hear a bird's song on a misty spring morning, we can "construct it"—hear it, appreciate it, understand it—in any number of ways. An ornithologist might supply an analytical framework about what that species of bird might be trying to achieve through that particular song in the circumstances of the microecosystem of that part of the forest. A musician might reflect on "found" music and ways in which the bird's song intersects with or diverges from other kinds of tonalities, rhythms, and musical idioms with which she is familiar in animal communication and human culture. Someone praying might be thankful for the blessings of creation made audible in the melody of the songbird, and from there be drawn deeper into adoration of the Creator. A supporter of animal rights might be moved to reflect on the mechanized brutality of factory farming and arrive at a sense of renewed commitment to ethical vegetarianism.

Countless interpretations of the bird's song are possible. Many different readings would be viable cultural productions for particular social and political circumstances. But the bird's song also has a purpose for the bird and for its "community"—other birds—whether the bird is fully cognizant of it or not. My interpretation may have little to do with what the song means to the bird. But the facts of the bird's existence and its singing are the indispensable basis for any scientific analysis, haiku, theological reflection, or meditation on birdliness that arises from encountering the birdsong. The "text" of the bird's song and the bird's practice of singing are not simply raw material for the construction of readers/hearers who come later. They are also to be honored as signifiers with their own integrity: as witnesses that are generative for all subsequent responses, however diverse and removed from the bird's own circumstances those responses might be.

Just so, the honoring of communicative intent in written texts may be as creative and far-reaching as the interpreter likes. Readers' constructions have never been and cannot be limited to original authorial intention. It is not even true that one *must* start with a sense of the author's apparent intent before moving on to new constructions of meaning. (That is the implication one discerns in some historical critics' work: they assume that every interpreter worth her salt will start with original intent, and then can go on to consider "contemporary applications" on her own time, once the primary and most important kind of interpretation—historical—has been done.) The act of reading is complex and takes place on multiple levels simultaneously. There is no way to "hear" a text naturally, or in one particular way, without prior assumptions, language structures, and social norms influencing our reading.

But honoring authorial intention as witness is an ethical imperative. If we are not to silence the actual people who spoke and wrote and edited the traditions of Scripture, we must acknowledge that their communicative strategies have meaning beyond what we may necessarily understand. How we honor those communicative strategies may differ depending on the type of communication, the type of literature, and the issues at stake for us in reading the piece of literature. For example, you might find historical authorial intent important when you are reading the book of Kings but almost impossible to ascertain when pondering a Japanese haiku. For the ancient political chronicle, one might seek to understand the author's view of events while placing that view in a larger context that relativizes and challenges its ideological limitations. For the haiku, one might seek to understand the poet's use of a traditional motif such as the evoking of silence or the mention of a particular color, or try to appreciate the tension between the formal syllabic constraints of the haiku form and the expansiveness of the poet's vision. The decisions we make about how to respond to texts are based on countless factors, including our own proclivities as interpreters and signals from texts or genres about openness to multiple interpretations. (The possibility of multiple readings is something a contemporary haiku writer might joyfully affirm and an ancient Deuteronomistic historian might vigorously dispute.) Textual forms, construction of authorial voice, use of stentorian pronouncement or ironic gesture or evocative metaphor: all these things cue the reader about how the author is trying to communicate meaning and how the author sees his or her own role in the act of bearing witness. To honor these things—whether agreeing or disagreeing, affirming or contesting or reframing—is a historical endeavor. Good historical analysis always acknowledges the situatedness of authors, textual forms and languages, and readers in particular historical contexts.

> "When a given text is read, simultaneously another text is also read, namely, the reader, or, perhaps better put, the life-experience of the reader of the text."
>
> —James W. Voelz, "Multiple Signs, Levels of Meaning and Self as Text: Elements of Intertextuality" (1995), 156

Historically based inquiry thus cannot be objective or natural. Texts are culturally freighted acts of communication, and the act of interpreting them is always shaped by the biases, values, assumptions, and judgments of the interpreter about every aspect of the text, the practice of reading, and the context of the interpreter. And let's not forget how complex each reader is, just on his or her own. As James Brenneman says, "Every reader is himself or herself a composite 'text' of sorts, full of already interpreted earlier texts."[1] The reader's own context is continually changing, too. Remember that novel that you thought was candid and achingly beautiful when you were a teenager but now find somewhat maudlin and predictable? Or that theological idea that left you cold when you first encountered it in the classroom, but that has since become a rich source of inspiration in your ministry? We change, and our reading changes too. To paraphrase Walt Whitman, every reader contains multitudes.

ARGUING OVER THE AUTHOR AND HISTORY

The dispute over authorial intent, or what is called (from the negative side) the "intentional fallacy," raged through English departments some decades ago, as postmodernism came into its own. The debate over the notion of author is now passé in those circles, although many critics continue to work tacitly with pragmatic notions of author. But the debate is alive and well in biblical studies, and rightly so, for a great deal is lost theologically and ethically if we do not wrestle with all of the implications and problems that attend the idea of author and its threatened loss. Impatience colors the conversation from both sides. Some postmodern thinkers become visibly irritated with historical critics, even those critics who attempt to articulate a nuanced view of history as a subtle and shifting complex of influences that may be understood from multiple perspectives. The view from the postmodern side of the methodological divide can be dogmatic and intolerant of historically oriented inquiries. Conversely, a good number of historical critics don't bother to acquaint themselves with postmodern ideas, dismissing "theory" as something artificial, secondary, and extraneous to the text. They do not understand that theory is (at its best) a thoughtful and elegant articulation of what various readers *already do* when they read and what texts may be doing—or trying to do—through their rhetorical strategies and literary artistry. In some quarters historical criticism is carried out as if postmodernism—as a complex multidisciplinary set of critiques of foundationalist, essentialist, and objectivist claims—had never happened or is of no account. On the other side, I have heard postmodern-leaning professors pronounce with relish that "historical criticism is dead," something that would come as quite a surprise to the historical critics who walk by me in the halls of Yale Divinity School every day. Historicists and postmodernists alike seem to

1. James Brenneman, *Canons in Conflict: Negotiating Texts in True and False Prophecy* (Oxford: Oxford University Press, 1997), 24.

be convinced that the *other* side enjoys the lion's share of institutional support and political power in the academy.

"Less than twenty years ago, it was still possible to pack most of the self-avowed postmodernists in biblical studies into a minivan. Where the minivan was headed on that occasion I do not remember. But I do recall one of its occupants advising the driver to be alert lest a gang of historical critics crammed into a bigger, meaner vehicle run us off the road, thereby ridding biblical studies of the scourge of postmodernism at a stroke. Those were heady days, giddy with self-aggrandizement, several of us being so naïve as to believe that historical criticism's stranglehold on the discipline would gradually and inexorably lessen as the acknowledged pillars and gatekeepers, comfortably sprawled in prestigious chairs in all the leading research universities, would retire or depart for the great senior common room in the sky, and be replaced with—well, postmodernists, of course, and other committed iconoclasts. How poorly we understood the rigid rules of dynastic succession that ensure the stability of our discipline through the generations."

—Stephen D. Moore, "A Modest Manifesto for New Testament Literary Criticism" (2007), 2

Postmodernists and historical critics often don't speak, smiling with a polite detachment as they pass each other in the halls of academe and avoiding each other's panels at national conferences. If you eavesdrop on conversations of the relevant groups, you learn that postmodernists tend to think of historical critics as benighted and completely unaware of the past several decades' worth of developments in literary theory—and, indeed, sometimes in historiographical theory as well. Hans M. Barstad gives voice to this view when he says, "To say that historians of ancient Israel are theory weak is, in my view, the understatement of the century. As a genre, most of the so-called 'histories of Israel' represent nothing more than various forms of a retelling of the biblical stories, diluted with sparse, desultory analytical remarks, not seldom with disparate references to 'archaeology.'"[2]

For their part, historical critics have trouble understanding why postmodernists do not see the need to allow historical context to govern interpretation in an authoritative way. My colleague John J. Collins frames this issue from the perspective of a traditional historian:

2. Hans M. Barstad, "History and the Hebrew Bible," in *Can a "History of Israel" Be Written?* ed. Lester L. Grabbe (Sheffield: Sheffield Academic Press, 1997), 46–47.

> Another assertion of at least some postmodern critics is that time is not an essential consideration in meaning. The fact that texts were composed long ago and in another place is not necessarily significant. Accordingly, postmodernists do not share the historical critic's dread of anachronism. Stephen Moore confesses, with disarming understatement, that "the avoidance of anachronism is not, perhaps, my strong suit as an exegete" as he proceeds to apply analogies from body-building to the biblical God. Yvonne Sherwood speaks of "hurling all kinds of contemporary idioms/preoccupations—all kinds of ropes of analogy—out to the shores of the ancient text in the hope that they will form some kind of attachment and in the process rearrange and reanimate the over-familiarised text." Whether one finds these far-flung analogies illuminating, entertaining, annoying, or infuriating, depends, I suppose, on where one's brain has been incubated or pickled.[3]

What's going on here? This is not just a matter of mild irritation at the clash of different writing styles. Something important is at stake. Traditional historians get quite angry at the apparent playfulness of postmodern language. Listen to John Barton on the subject of the whimsy of postmodern readings:

> I find postmodernism absurd, rather despicable in its delight in debunking all serious beliefs, decadent and corrupt in its indifference to questions of truth; I do not believe in it for a moment. But as a game, a set of *jeux d'esprit*, a way of having fun with words, I find it diverting and entertaining: I enjoy the absurd and the surreal, and postmodernism supplies [those] in ample measure. Postmodernist theory is like postmodernist knitting. You begin to make a sock, but having turned the heel you continue with a neckband; then you add two (or three) arms of unequal length, and finish not by casting off but simply by removing the needles, so that the whole garment slowly unravels. Provided you don't want to *wear* a postmodern garment, nothing could be more entertaining. But when the knitter tells us that garments don't really exist anyway, we should probably suspend our belief in postmodernist theory, and get back to our socks.[4]

Wow—this is serious business! Barton seems to be conflicted: one moment he confesses to finding postmodernism diverting, but in the next moment, he calls it absurd, despicable, decadent, and corrupt. What's at stake here is that postmodern modes of engagement present a sharp challenge to the post-Enlightenment Western privileging of a certain kind of history. Some who are intellectually invested in traditional historical positivism are clearly affronted by the challenge.

3. John J. Collins, *The Bible after Babel: Historical Criticism in a Postmodern Age* (Grand Rapids: Wm. B. Eerdmans Pub. Co., 2005), 15.

4. John Barton, *Reading the Old Testament: Method in Biblical Study* (Louisville, KY: Westminster John Knox Press, 1996), 235, with original emphasis.

Not a few historical critics enjoy highlighting convoluted sentences in postmodern writing as if the ideas engaged there were obviously risible simply because the language is hard to follow. Here's the kind of sentence that a traditional modernist scholar might mock: "One should not force experiential reality into a procrustean bed of homogenising logic and believe that this procedure has exhausted all epistemic possibilities, but neither should one merely juxtapose all perspectives, pastiche-like, believing that cognitive or ontological fragmentation, and hence relativism . . . is the best one can do."[5] The sentence is actually perfectly intelligible, but it might take a little work to decode it if the reader is not used to thinking about epistemology (analysis of the ways in which we know) or is not familiar with the concept of "pastiche" in poststructuralist thought. To be fair to those who disparage poststructuralism, here's a sentence that is quite hard to understand, from French philosopher Gilles Deleuze: "What is neither individual nor personal are, on the contrary, emissions of singularities insofar as they occur on an unconscious surface and possess a mobile, immanent principle of auto-unification through a *nomadic distribution*, radically distinct from fixed and sedentary distributions as conditions of the syntheses of consciousness."[6] Or again, recently I consulted an article that uses "matrixing" as a gerund. Now, I would have put money on the fact that "matrixing" is not a word in the English language, but there you go.

Yet every discipline has its technical language. I interpret historical critics' impatience with literary-critical jargon as, at least in part, anxiety about the looming threat of interdisciplinary incompetence: it makes most of us nervous to come across standards and criteria for excellence that we ourselves would not be equipped to meet. It's noteworthy that biblical historical critics tend to be not at all disparaging about the intricacies of comparative Northwest Semitic linguistics, even though that set of jargon terms and technical skills is certainly no more accessible to the uninitiated than are the terminology and analytical skills employed in poststructuralist circles.

These issues, arcane though they might sound, do affect how pastors and other ministers treat the Bible in their sermons, parish discussion groups, and other venues. Preachers sometimes stall in the place of being alert to historical-critical discussions of their texts but unsure of how to proclaim the gospel in a way that enlivens the congregation's appreciation of the ancient context without sounding like they are reading dry-as-dust history homework out loud. Postmodern readers may be captivated by the elusiveness and

5. Bert Olivier, "Nature as 'Abject,' Critical Psychology, and 'Revolt': The Pertinence of Kristeva," *South African Journal of Psychology* 37 (2007): 445.

6. Gilles Deleuze, *The Logic of Sense*, trans. Mark Lester (New York: Columbia University Press, 1990), 102.

"thickness" of situated readings, but not be quite sure how to engage the theological dimensions of the text for communities that cherish the Bible as Scripture.

In this chapter, we will wade into the thick of the arguments about historical, literary, and ideological criticism of biblical texts. These discussions are designed to help you think theologically about your own practices of reading and the practices of reading that you want to model and teach in your congregation or in whatever context you work. My hopes here are two. First, I hope that readers from across the spectrum of beliefs and convictions about texts and reading will see that multiple approaches to the biblical text can yield theological fruit of varied and beautiful kinds. Second, I hope that neither staunchly historicist readers nor adamantly postmodern readers will be able to ignore each other's positions. A politics of mutual dismissal would mean many missed opportunities for the academy and for the church. Only when we engage with generosity these disputes over meaning and intention can we come to a nuanced appreciation of the complexity of interpretation, taking into account the ethical value of ancient witness, the extraordinary power of literary artistry, and the importance of astuteness about ideological dimensions of texts, rhetoric, and hermeneutical models.

Two brief excursuses will prepare us for this journey. First, we'll think about the prior assumptions and intuitions that we bring to the act of reading, and second, we'll consider the role of tradition in shaping our hermeneutical imagination.

PRIOR ASSUMPTIONS AND INTUITIONS

What assumptions do we bring to the interpretation of texts? How do we frame questions of literary meaning and the approaches that are likely to yield fruit? Do we tend to assume that texts are true unless proved otherwise? Do we value well-constructed, reasoned arguments over passionate stream-of-consciousness musings about a subject, or do we respond more to visionary rhetoric and dramatic metaphors than to accurate but dry technical points? Each reader's answers to these questions will vary depending on the text being read, the purposes for which the reader is reading it, and the temperament that the reader brings to the interpretive endeavor. One reader might be intrigued by the details in an operations manual for a computer and pore over every page, while another wouldn't dream of reading a single section of that manual unless it were absolutely necessary for pragmatic reasons. One reader might be lost for hours in the evocative images and powerful silences of a poem, whereas another might be frustrated by the lack of clarity in the same poem and throw the book of poetry across the room. One reader might be fascinated by the polemical ideological biases in a piece of ancient history writing and delight in deconstructing it, while another might look earnestly to the same literature for ethical or moral guidance in contemporary life.

I pause to observe that excellent work has been done on temperament differences in human beings. Two tools for measuring temperament difference have found wide use in theological education and in the church: the Myers-Briggs Type Indicator and the Enneagram.[7] If every theological faculty and every theological student were guided in reflecting on those tools and the diversity of temperaments they highlight, we'd have a far deeper understanding of some of the sources of friction in theological, methodological, and interpersonal disputes.

John Barton suggests that scholarly interpretive methods may be best understood as "a codification of intuitions about the text which may occur to intelligent readers."[8] All readers bring particular strategies, intuitions, information, and assumptions to the biblical text, and there are many ways of being an intelligent reader. It is not the case that untrained readers read "naturally" or simply whereas scholars read in an artificially complicated or technical way. Rather, scholars are required by their academic disciplines to articulate clearly the assumptions with which they are working when they read. Some scholars are able to articulate their own strategies, intuitions, and assumptions better than others. Unfortunately, one can still easily find a scholarly book that reads as if the author's perspective were the only reasonable view and the author's method were the transparently logical choice for illuminating the text. Be that as it may, we should recognize that the average person in the pew brings plenty of assumptions to the biblical text as well. Often, she or he has simply not had the opportunity to examine those assumptions in a critical and self-aware way. To those who are inclined to dismiss scholarly interpretations as too ivory-tower or abstract, and to those who are inclined to dismiss untrained readers' interpretations as too simplistic or uninformed, I would say alike: all reader responses matter.

It is often said that an understanding of genre is a crucial element in intelligent reading. This is certainly true. The purposes of lists, novels, annual

7. For the Myers-Briggs Type Indicator and related discussions, see David Keirsey and Marilyn Bates, *Please Understand Me: Character and Temperament Types* (Del Mar, CA: Prometheus Nemesis, 1984); and David Keirsey, *Please Understand Me II: Temperament, Character, Intelligence* (Del Mar, CA: Prometheus Nemesis, 1998). Information on the Enneagram may be found at http://www.enneagraminstitute.com/. Among the many books on the Enneagram are Don Richard Riso and Russ Hudson, *The Wisdom of the Enneagram: The Complete Guide to Psychological and Spiritual Growth for the Nine Personality Types* (New York: Bantam Books, 1999); Richard Rohr and Andreas Ebert, *The Enneagram: A Christian Perspective*, trans. Peter Heinegg (New York: Crossroad, 2009).

8. Barton, *Reading the Old Testament*, 5.

reports of corporations, spiritual reflections, e-mails to family, volumes of systematic theology, and newspaper articles are all quite diverse. It would be a mark of reader incompetence (or poor writing on the part of the author) if one mistook one of those forms for another and misread it. But competent genre identification is only part of the task of reading. Several other factors are crucially important for one to navigate literary works—and one's own expectations of them—with intellectual rigor, grace, and sophistication. One must understand one's own temperament and be aware, at least in part, of what one is looking for when one reads a particular work of literature. One should try to understand the genre conventions and purposes communicated by the author of a work, noting that those conventions and purposes might be very complex indeed.

There are many assumptions, explicit and hidden, that guide and shape our interpretive efforts. No reading of a text is neutral or free from prior assumptions. If a reader suggests that the prophet Jonah was literally swallowed by a large fish, she may be assuming that the book of Jonah is a straightforward, realistic piece of historical reportage. That is not a "natural" assumption, because there were many different kinds of literature in ancient times—just as there are today—and there is no neutral or natural reason why the book of Jonah should be assumed to be straightforward historiography rather than, say, a parable containing obviously fantastical elements for instructive purposes or an ironic short story whose overall point is political.

THE ROLE OF TRADITION

Even a quick glance at the history of interpretation will show how wondrously rich and varied are the biblical readings that have been offered in Christian tradition. Each reading has its own value for a particular social, political, or ecclesial circumstance, and each has its own flaws and limitations. To see a brilliant demonstration of this, take a look at Yvonne Sherwood's survey of the history of interpretation of Jonah, *A Biblical Text and Its Afterlives: The Survival of Jonah in Western Culture* (Cambridge University Press, 2000), which explores many fascinating interpretations of Jonah in rabbinic, Christian, and secular contexts over the centuries. Every act of interpretation is a choice, or actually a whole complex of interconnected choices, about how to construe the evidence and frame the questions that one poses to the text.

Some ecclesial reading communities expect a strict adherence to their particular denomination's characteristic way of reading, or they might privilege the authority of the denomination's teachings as a dominant factor in the individual's encounters with Scripture. Other ecclesial reading communities privilege the individual's encounter with Scripture as something that may be guided anew by the Holy Spirit apart from the weight of previous centuries of church doctrine. These traditions shape our interpretive imaginations, sometimes constraining the possibilities and "ruling out" certain approaches, other times inviting readers into deep and mysterious depths.

I encourage you to remember that not all representations of a tradition's views on Scripture may be accurate. An ecclesial leader or biblical scholar may pronounce, "Well, our tradition has always read Scripture *this* way," but such a pronouncement may betray the expert's own biases more than the church's, or may not take adequate account of the full history of interpretation. Churches tend to think that the way in which they have done things for the past eighty years or so—that is, in the living memory of those who are currently there—is the way that things have *always* been done. It is also the case that some aspects of tradition simply should not be allowed to continue unchallenged. Racism has marred the history of many churches in North America up until, and even beyond, the civil rights movement in this country; yet obviously, implicit and overt racist practices should not go unchallenged. Many theological schools in North America have discerned the importance of examining theological curricula for evidence of androcentric and racial bias. Our syllabi should no longer be restricted to the works of white Euro-American male scholars; the fact that education has for so long allowed the continuing suppression of other voices demonstrates a large-scale and disastrous failure of cultural imagination that should be remedied in a whole variety of creative ways. Or again, many laywomen have provided profound and intelligent readings of Scripture over the centuries. But because laywomen's intellectual learning was not always promoted or supported in various social contexts and because women were outright excluded from scholastic academies until relatively recently, their contributions have not generally been valued as highly as those of male clerics. This practice, too, should not be allowed to pass any longer without comment and remedy.

Tradition itself can be impoverished or misunderstood by its own adherents. Some years ago, I made a presentation on Jeremiah to a group of Roman Catholic seminarians at a seminary with a reputation for theological conservatism. A student objected to my suggestion, which is standard in biblical scholarship, that the book of Jeremiah had been edited by later scribes. He said, "You say it was edited, but *we* [he meant Roman Catholics] believe the book of Jeremiah was written entirely by the historical man Jeremiah." The student was ignorant of the text of Jeremiah itself, which often speaks of Jeremiah in the third person and never makes the claim that the entire book was penned by the prophet. He was also ignorant of the early church's alertness to different kinds of material within the book of Jeremiah, recent Roman Catholic teachings on biblical hermeneutics, and the contributions of many Roman Catholic scholars to redaction-critical scholarship. His assertion about what "we believe" was not, in fact, even remotely accurate. The ecclesial traditions of particular communities are often much more diverse in history and in contemporary practice than their members may realize.

So it matters that we consider not only the content of what we read, but also how what we read is influenced by our assumptions about the text, interpretive strategies, and the history and priorities of interpretive communities that have shaped us. Consider the following subjective factors, each construed in myriad ways by different interpreters as they read any given text in the Bible:

- *The historical context(s) that gave rise to the production of the biblical text.* Understanding what historical influences and factors were at play in the shaping of texts can be notoriously difficult for ancient contexts about which we may have little information. It can be tricky even for a current historical context about which we have a great deal of information. Consider the long-term political infighting among various Cambodian diaspora groups backing different leaders from the 1980s to the present day; the desperate economic situation in Haiti in the aftermath of the Duvalier regime; or the competing causes and rationales offered for the United States' war in Iraq starting in 2003. Even with plenty of information at our disposal, analysts can come up with strikingly different understandings of what has happened and what is at stake.
- *The relationship between historical context and textual representation.* Some interpreters write as if there were a transparent relationship between major political events in a given historical period and the biblical literature that was composed or edited during that time. This assumption is flawed. Did every novel or poem or liturgy or memo composed in 2010 reflect what was going on at the top levels of government in the nations in which those authors lived? Of course not. Even if we concede that textual production was more limited in ancient Israel and was more closely controlled by those in political power, it is nevertheless true that numerous cultural, political, spiritual, and artistic factors have always affected the production of texts and their meanings.
- *Literary aspects of meaning in texts*, that is, the semantic meanings of words, metaphors, and similes; the importance of genre; hidden meanings conveyed by irony, sarcasm, and other forms of misdirection; and so forth. Meaning is created by interactions in a huge variety of factors within and outside of texts, and all of these are then construed in particular ways by the interpreter. The intertextual and intercultural web of associations and resonances becomes so rich and multilayered that for many postmodernists, meaning in any strictly constrained sense is infinitely "deferred" and can never be fully decided.

Readers who consider the above dimensions of the interpretive task well will be able to offer more nuanced and profound interpretations in their sermons, Bible teaching, and scholarship.

A major disagreement in foundational assumptions underlies arguments between modernist and postmodernist readers. Modernist reading strategies have tended to assume certain kinds of starting points for interpretation. Some would aver that an understanding of the historical context in which a text was written is indispensable for interpretation; such historical contexts usually assume some kind of interest in authorial intent. Others have argued that we cannot fully know the historical context or the mind of an author, so the only viable starting place for interpretation is "the text itself" as an aesthetic object. Still others have insisted on ethical or theological considerations as a foundational starting point for interpretation: the Bible can be interpreted best when it is interpreted in accord with church teaching over the centuries, say, or biblical texts must be read with a feminist lens that inquires into the potentially oppressive and potentially liberatory aspects of each text's message. All of these modernist approaches—themselves far more diverse than can be sketched briefly here—have been confronted by the antifoundationalist emphases of a variety of postmodernist ways of reading. Postmodernist hermeneutical strategies, too, are far too diverse to be summed up easily, but they tend to position themselves critically over against foundationalist and essentialist claims, preferring to see particular readings as local responses influenced by a host of readerly commitments and cultural assumptions encoded in the context(s) in which the reader is working.

What interests me here is one particular site of struggle within the lively clashes of countless ways of reading: the arguments between historically minded scholars and radical constructionists. Historical scholars fearing the specter of "relativism" often give little credence to radical-constructionist views of meaning in their writings and in their classrooms. Depending on what seminary or divinity school a student attends, that student may never even hear that there are vast and lively areas of biblical scholarship that do not take traditional historical inquiry as their starting point. For their part, radical constructionists often do not acknowledge inconsistencies in their own reading practices and what may be lost theologically when readers of Scripture move entirely away from authorial intent and textual constraints on meaning.

In what follows, I will explore some basic tenets and pragmatic workings of major methodological orientations to Scripture and reflect on some of the theological implications that I see, with a particular eye to guiding readers into the argument between historical and postmodernist ways of reading. This is not intended as a comprehensive treatment of interpretive methods. There are many introductions to method available, from tomes about evangelical hermeneutics to historical-critical handbooks to collections of essays on postmodern methodologies.[9] The observations that follow are intended as an introductory guide to what is at stake theologically in the application of various approaches.

As we go, keep in mind that while varied reading strategies can enrich and supplement each other, there are ways in which the basic assumptions of different methodologies are fundamentally incompatible. It is not the case that one may pick up any number of "tools"—methods—and wield them simultaneously or seriatim with no ill consequences. The popular metaphor of "toolbox" is inadequate when we are talking about interpretive strategies. "Toolbox" would work well as a metaphor only if we meant that the hammer in the toolbox keeps hitting the screwdriver and bending it out of shape so that it can't do its job (or must envision its job in new ways), and the very existence of symmetry and an objective plumb is disputed by the hacksaw, to the irritation of the carpenter's level. Keep in mind also that as methods become more familiar, they will not "mean" in the same way that they did when they first arrived on the interpretive scene. The same kind of historical criticism that was once found to be innovative and dangerous by ecclesial authorities is now standard—and many would say, still dominant—in the academy; it has become the new "authority" that must be challenged. Once-sharp challenges to modernist notions of text and author are now old hat for those who have kept up with developments in literary criticism in English departments. Settings matter, too. That textual indeterminacy invites competing readings is so obvious as to go without saying these days at the annual meeting of the Modern Language Association. But as regards the potential multivalence of Scripture, this would be brand-new news—perhaps exciting, perhaps shocking—to many folks in the pews of our local churches.

9. For readers who would like to peruse books on interpretive method, here are some representative examples. One handbook for evangelical hermeneutics is William W. Klein, Craig L. Blomberg, and Robert L. Hubbard Jr., *Introduction to Biblical Interpretation* (Dallas: Word, 1993). Two books tacitly grounded in historical-critical approaches to Scripture are John H. Hayes and Carl R. Holladay, *Biblical Exegesis: A Beginner's Handbook*, 3rd ed. (Louisville, KY: Westminster John Knox Press, 2007); and Barton, *Reading the Old Testament* (see note 4 above). A book that focuses on literary-critical strategies and postmodern interpretation is Steven L. McKenzie and Stephen R. Haynes, eds., *To Each Its Own Meaning: An Introduction to Biblical Criticisms and Their Application*, rev. and expanded ed. (Louisville, KY: Westminster John Knox Press, 1999). A book that attends closely to the implications of postmodernism for biblical interpretation is The Bible and Culture Collective, *The Postmodern Bible* (New Haven, CT: Yale University Press, 1995). For general orientation to foundational texts in postmodernist theory, see Joseph Natoli and Linda Hutcheon, eds., *A Postmodern Reader* (Albany: State University of New York Press, 1993).

> "Trumpeting the death of the author and evincing a penchant for deconstructive reading may once have had you marked as a dangerous anarchist; the same behaviour in English departments today is just as likely to render you nothing more threatening than an expounder of the boringly obvious, and this is because poststructuralist theories have been with us long enough to have become domesticated, to have coalesced into a snug critical position which can be settled into with satisfaction and ease. At the brink of the abyss of non-signification, at the very limit of thought itself, there now sits an armchair and a coffee table stacked with well-thumbed back issues of Diacritics."
>
> —David Rutledge, in "Faithful Reading: Poststructuralism and the Sacred" (1996), 274

HISTORICAL INQUIRY

Biblical historical criticism in the Western academy arose in significant part as a corrective to the way in which dogmatic positions were enforced within the Christian church about what Bible texts should mean. Scholars of biblical history applied what they saw as rational, objective criteria for assessing evidence (textual and archaeological) having to do with the time periods in which the Bible was composed. Intense arguments flared in the last part of the twentieth century about the ideas of "biblical history" and "biblical archaeology." Some scholars argued cogently that for truly historical study to go forward, as opposed to Christian apologetics with a historical flavor, interpreters must consider ancient Near Eastern history and Syro-Palestinian archaeology as independent disciplines, the Bible being simply one cultural product to be examined along with extrabiblical evidence. I will attend in more detail to issues of history writing and historical analysis in chapter 3. For now, we will think about some of the issues involved in the debate among historical critics, literary critics, and postmodernists.

What are the critiques that one may level against biblical historical inquiry, or at least, historical inquiry naively performed? Many serious problems beset historically oriented types of interpretation that do not reflect careful thought about the complexities of textual representation and awareness of reader agency. Here are three problems with biblical historical inquiry that is poorly thought through and unnuanced.

1. *Historical critics are sometimes unduly influenced by the views of those who wielded political power in the societies under investigation.* One can pick up a history book—whether a scholarly tome or an elementary-school textbook—and

gain the impression that the important events in history mainly concern rulers, wars, religious leaders, and the monumental architecture and monumental devastation that rulers and wars leave behind. This is far from true. Real life for the vast majority of human beings is not bound up in any direct and reportable way with the outcomes of particular elections (or coups) and battles, except insofar as rulers and wars create economic and social stability or instability that can be experienced at the local level. But those in positions of political and military power present the important events of human life in those terms. Often the perspectives of those without money or land (the poor, and even the not-wealthy), women, and others who have been kept from positions at the center of public power structures have not been well represented in the writing of national historical narratives. Too often historians have uncritically accepted those large-scale military and political priorities as "natural" ones around which to arrange our stories about cultures and peoples.

It is often said that history is written by the victors. Though that statement is a bit too simplistic, it is unquestionably true that those with power try, through all the means at their disposal, to dominate the priorities for cultural representation of what is important in their own times. Scholars should not absorb the priorities of an elite few in an unthinking manner when formulating their own questions for critical historical inquiry. It is not true that wars, reigns of particular kings, and the construction of large palaces and statues are necessarily the most important things to remember about peoples and their cultures. Yet that is the impression we inevitably receive from historical books that provide charts of kings' reigns and maps of military movements but no information on methods of childbearing and the education of children, the average lifespan of women (which in many cultures differs significantly from the average lifespan of men), forms of popular religious practice rather than officially sanctioned ritual, ways in which ancient societies practiced charity and care for the poor, and so on. Although historians have brought critically informed perspectives to bear on the variables within the larger picture framed by rulers and wars, too seldom have they critiqued that very way of framing history. I learned much about the history of "official" Israelite religion, battles, and the checkered histories of the Israelite and Judean monarchies during my master's and doctoral work in the Hebrew Scriptures, but women's roles in domestic and public culture and childbearing came up virtually not at all in five years of coursework.[10]

10. One class on Gen. 21 addressed, literally for about 90 seconds, the weaning age of children in ancient Israel. In the master's-level introductory course, we spent about 20 minutes on feminist biblical criticism, using readings from the 1970s even though the class took place in 1991. Otherwise, women's bodies, women's roles in ancient Israel, cultural analyses of the femi-

Official pronouncements on religion and officially authorized forms of cultic practice may dominate historical records, but the beliefs and worship lives of countless people and communities throughout history often did not conform entirely, or even chiefly, to official prescriptions. When we allow our imaginations to be constrained by the priorities of royalty, court officials, clergy, and military leaders, we risk losing our sensitivity to vast and rich portions of human life in community, portions *not* dictated by monarchs, clerics, and army strongmen. The production of culture in any time period and any region is due to a host of complex, interrelated factors. Historians in recent decades have vigorously challenged the way in which historiography had been practiced, with its unblinking focus on metanarratives. Since the advent of New Historicism, the Western practice of historical analysis has increasingly incorporated attention to the idiosyncratic, the popular (as versus the official), and the local.

2. *Historical critics sometimes confuse the views of biblical characters and narrators with what may have actually happened in history*. Biblical texts, as literature, are complex regarding their presentation of "point of view" within narratives, the relationships they portray among characters, and their performances of narratorial and character voicing. Too often historical critics read biblical texts, including texts that are clearly not historiographical in nature, as if they reflected situations in history directly or with just a thin veneer of fictionalization. Here's an example. Consider the text in Genesis in which Abraham says that he thought there was "no fear of God at all" in the Egyptian court; the patriarch figures that Sarah should lie and say that she is his sister rather than his wife (Gen. 20:11), so that the godless Egyptians do not kill him in order to take her. Some contemporary commentators simply reproduce the viewpoint that the Egyptian court was godless and ruthless, as if it were not only the biblical narrator's view (which I am convinced it is not) but also the historically verifiable truth about the ethos and morality of the Egyptian court in that time. David J. A. Clines offers an acid comment about a similar tendency in commentaries on Amos to assume that the situation described rhetorically in the text mirrors reality:

> How can we possibly know whether the poverty portrayed in Amos was widespread; how can we know whether the rich were in some way responsible for the poverty of the poor or whether there was some structural cause, which was really no one individual's fault, for the poverty of a minority? . . . We cannot simply assume that a prosperous society owes its prosperity to the deprivation of its poor. You couldn't say that about modern Switzerland, for example. Should

nine in biblical and contemporary texts, and gender criticism (including critical engagement of masculinity as such) came up not even once during my five full-time years of study.

> not biblical commentators have to do a course in economics before they deliver themselves of opinions about Israelite society that they proffer in their own voice? Certainly, they shouldn't be allowed to parrot the prophets and pretend they are doing scholarly analysis.[11]

In a word: biblical historical critics can be startlingly naive about the relationship between text and context, missing the subtleties with which literary texts use misdirection, conflicting viewpoints, irony, and other artful means to tell stories.

3. *Historical critics sometimes seem unaware of their own cultural and epistemological biases.* History as a field of inquiry has not privileged (or necessarily even respected) modes of inquiry that are self-reflective and that train practitioners in modes of awareness about their own cultural, emotional, and sociopsychological issues. Biblical historical critics often bring their own issues and prejudices to the subject in a way that is markedly less self-aware than one might find in other disciplines such as pastoral care, a discipline in which self-awareness about personal and methodological biases is regularly addressed, or Christian education, wherein different modes of learning and types of processing information are explicitly explored and analyzed. Are there practitioners in every field of scholarly inquiry who are unaware of their own biases, prejudices, and commitments? Sure. But biblical historical inquiry, as it has traditionally been formulated, has made something of a fetish out of purportedly "neutral" and "objective" scholarship, dismissing the biases and values of the historian as irrelevant. Bracketing one's own opinions is one thing. Pretending one's own biases do not exist is quite another, and that latter approach has been a hallmark of biblical historical-critical scholarship in many quarters.

These days many interpretive models acknowledge the impossibility of reading as if we had no biases or prior commitments. Biblical historical critics, however, are proving themselves to be among the last to concede this point. Ways of reading that do not take into account one's own prejudices—even on issues such as what constitutes a text or an author—can yield readings of Scripture that are significantly out of focus. Consider the critique of historical criticism offered by James A. Sanders, a biblical scholar who has pressed interpreters to see Scripture texts as having been shaped over time in living communities rather than by single authors and later editors:

> Historical criticism in its handling of the Bible has bypassed the ancient communities that produced it and shaped it. It has focused, in good modern Western fashion, on individual authors. Liberals

11. David J. A. Clines, "Metacommentating Amos," in *Of Prophets' Visions and the Wisdom of Sages: Essays in Honour of R. Norman Whybray on His Seventieth Birthday*, ed. Heather A. McKay and David J. A. Clines (Sheffield: JSOT Press, 1993), 148–49.

> and conservatives alike have done the same: the one simply attributes less of a text to the early "author" than the other. . . . And historical criticism has been primitivist, locking the Bible into the past, even decanonizing it thereby, as [Gerald] Sheppard has aptly put it. And criticism has in large measure tended to fragmentize the text, though redaction criticism has corrected the tendency to some extent. Finally, criticism has felt free to rewrite the text in the light of . . . an effort to reconstruct an Urtext [original or earliest text]. Rewriting the Bible with such conviction caused a shift of locus of authority from what the early believing communities received, shaped, and passed on, to what scholars were convinced was said or written in the first place.[12]

"Since for historical criticism the text as means possessed a univocal and objective meaning and since this could be retrieved via a properly informed and conducted scientific inquiry, the meaning uncovered was for all times and cultures. . . . The historical paradigm was remarkably inbred and thoroughly hegemonic. The theoretical discussion, such as it was, consisted mostly of an in-house affair conducted within certain well-established parameters: acquaintance with the various stages of historical criticism, and a reading of previous exegesis on the area of research in question. Dialogue with other critical models and disciplines was largely nonexistent."

—Fernando F. Segovia, *Decolonizing Biblical Studies* (2000), 14–15

What are the theological risks of a simplistic kind of historicism? We risk profoundly underestimating the rich complexity of sacred traditions. We risk mishearing the ancient witnesses of individuals and communities that struggled, warred, and perhaps even died for the sake of the theological testimony they wanted to leave behind. We risk importing the cultural blinders and new prejudices of our own age into a text that is far more mysterious and elusive than clear.

But historical-critical inquiry has contributed enormously to the knowledge we have of ancient cultures and ancient literary traditions. Historical criticism has put a needed check on the uncritical replication of Christian dogma in texts and traditions that may originally have had little or nothing to do with later theological developments. This is not to say that ecclesially oriented readings and theologically freighted readings are now to be dismissed as useless. But it does require that we think carefully about our own

12. James A. Sanders, *From Sacred Story to Sacred Text: Canon as Paradigm* (Philadelphia: Fortress Press, 1987), 163.

"situatedness" when we read Scripture so that we don't read with an uncritical narcissism, as if our own personal or cultural norms and beliefs were speaking in these texts that were written millennia ago in radically different cultural contexts. Scripture should challenge us as well as strengthen us. The message of Amos will be diluted and distorted if we read him as if he were a twenty-first-century liberal Protestant. The theological impact of the book of Isaiah will be muted and deformed if we assume that Isaiah's perspective regarding the authority of ancient tradition mirrors the position taken by the Roman Catholic Church with regard to the magisterium. In other words, historical criticism can be excellent for helping us to see the situatedness of all cultural expressions. It is just that, as traditionally practiced, historical criticism has been reluctant to identify and examine its *own* biases and cultural prejudices.

LITERARY CRITICISM

Literary approaches to Scripture are wonderfully diverse and include a plethora of subdisciplines: narrative criticism, form and genre criticism, structuralism, rhetorical criticism, studies of intertextuality, poetic analysis, and much more. Any good handbook of method will elucidate the assumptions and working strategies of those methods. What literary approaches have in common is the assumption that the literary features of the biblical text matter. A text's artistry, compositional structures, development of characters and plot, use of discourse and silence, manipulation of genre expectations, and employment of metaphors, imagery, and irony are not just aesthetic window dressing for the underlying ideas of the text. Rather, these literary dimensions are essential to the ways in which the text invites meaning-making.

This point is important, because some traditional historical scholars tend to treat literary questions as secondary or peripheral concerns. For example, an unnuanced historical reading could propose that the book of Ruth simply reflects the position that other ethnic groups were welcome within Israel. Boring! Or let me put my objection in a more nuanced way. While that may be true at least in part, if the historical reading does not attend carefully to the marvelous ambiguities of plot and characterization within the book of Ruth, it will drastically oversimplify the ways in which the text addresses itself to questions of ethnicity and belonging. A naive historical reading of a character in Scripture may fall far short of illuminating the subject if it does not take subtleties of characterization, plot development, and the larger literary structure of the relevant biblical book into account. For a historian to propose that Samson, for example, is just a typical charismatic leader in premonarchical Israel (yawn!) would be to ignore the literary subtleties artfully employed in the deeply ambivalent characterization of Samson and the gradually intensifying larger-scale ironies in the book of Judges that serve to undermine the role of judge more and more as the book careens to its horrific conclusion. Literary considerations are not aesthetic afterthoughts that can be separated from the analysis of a text's purported historical core. The "literariness" of narratives, the elliptical artistry of biblical poetry, and the condensed aphoristic form of biblical wisdom sayings are integral means by which those texts communicate and invite interpretation.

Let's briefly consider three aspects of the literary nature of biblical texts: character, metaphor, and irony. A heightened awareness of these literary features of texts can lead not only to a fuller appreciation of the power of Scripture as literature but also to important theological implications for the ways in which readers understand their spiritual imaginations as being addressed by Scripture.

Character

Characters in Hebrew Bible narratives are often sketched sparingly. They are usually portrayed in terms of their actions rather than their personal histories, feelings, and political or ideological commitments. There are some notable exceptions to this. We are allowed to see the turbulent emotions that rack Joseph when his brothers finally meet him in the Egyptian court. The brushstrokes with which the Succession Narrative writers paint the psyches and motivations of Saul, Jonathan, David, and Bathsheba are expertly subtle. Jonah's frustration and rage are significant for his story; the mental anguish and despair suffered by Job and by "the Preacher" of Ecclesiastes are narrated in exquisite detail. But generally, we learn more about what biblical characters do in their interactions with other people and with God than what has shaped or motivated them as characters. The biblical text's attentiveness to characters' actions invites us to consider carefully the complex ways in which events shape both local outcomes and the longer-term destiny of a family or tribe, a community, the people of Israel writ large, or all of the nations. We never learn whether Abram is afraid, curious, courageous, or confused when he hears God's call to go from Ur to a new land (Gen. 12:1–3), but we do hear that his decision to obey will have consequences both for those descended from him and for all the families of the earth in their relationships with his offspring. Later, when Abraham raises his hand to slay his beloved son Isaac, we hear nothing of his or Isaac's feelings, but we know what had happened before—that Abraham and Sarah had waited for many decades to have their own son and had feared that God's promises to them would not be fulfilled. The actions of that drama in Genesis 22 play out against a background that is thunderous with the unspoken.

"The two of them, Isaac carrying the wood and Abraham with fire and a knife, 'went together.' Hesitantly, Isaac ventures to ask about the ram, and Abraham gives the well-known answer. Then the text repeats, 'So they went both of them together.' Everything remains unexpressed. . . . The decisive points of the narrative alone are emphasized, what lies between is nonexistent; time and place are undefined and call for interpretation; thoughts and feeling remain unexpressed, are only suggested by the silence and the fragmentary speeches; the whole permeated with the most unrelieved suspense and directed toward a single goal (and to that extent far more of a unity), remains mysterious and 'fraught with background.'"

—Erich Auerbach, "Odysseus' Scar," in *Mimesis* (1953), 9

We could dismiss the spareness of characterization in ancient Israelite literature as merely a by-product of a particular set of cultural norms in literature. But more can be said. The choice of theologian Augustine of Hippo (354–430) to write in the soul-bearing voice of "spiritual autobiography" was a significant moment in the history of theological literature, with important implications for the ways in which theological "subjects" could learn how to articulate their subjectivity in the spiritual encounter with God. So too, the ways in which the Hebrew Scriptures treat characters matters for what those texts are communicating. Theologically, we see in the way in which Hebrew Bible stories portray characters that actions situate the characters in the life of a community and serve to advance or frustrate community-building in line with the purposes of God.

What about character development? This is portrayed in extraordinarily refined and easy-to-miss ways in Hebrew Scripture narrative. Biblical scholar Meir Sternberg suggests that ancient Hebrew narrative employs a subtle

> strategy of disclosure whereby the given does not suffice and the sufficient is not given in time or at all. In its application to character portrayal, this strategy manifests itself in a distributed, often oblique and tortuous unfolding of features. So reading a character becomes a process of discovery, attended by all the biblical hallmarks: progressive reconstruction, tentative closure of discontinuities, frequent and sometimes painful reshaping in the face of the unexpected, and intractable pockets of darkness to the very end.[13]

13. Meir Sternberg, *The Poetics of Biblical Narrative: Ideological Literature and the Drama of Reading* (Bloomington: Indiana University Press, 1985), 323–24.

We learn from Sternberg that it is not enough just to read a character superficially, looking for qualities on the surface of the story. We need to take account of the character as experienced in the full unfolding of a story, with its closures and lack of closures, its overt gestures toward character and its silences. Does this approach to reading the Bible sound too scholarly or technical? It really isn't. This kind of reading, toward a fuller understanding of character and of the text generally, is possible for any Scripture reader who is willing to read *all* of Scripture—or at least, all of a relevant biblical book—rather than just dipping in for isolated verses or glancing at favorite stories taken out of context. Short lectionary snippets or Bible studies in which a story is read in isolation are simply not adequate for a full appreciation of the artistry and theological power of Scripture. (That's why in the electronic Bible study forum that I lead, we always read whole biblical books, not just sections or isolated stories.[14]) The more Scripture you know well, the more adept you will become at perceiving a significant silence in the way a story is told or not told, a nuanced reversal of expectations in the larger sweep of a book's plot, or the creative elaboration of a particular ancient motif or tradition.

Metaphor

Metaphors are powerful ways of structuring our cultural imaginations. Through the establishing of a connection between unlike things, each metaphor brings a host of associations into close relationship, leaving us with vivid impressions of a truth that seems to be both new and familiar. Making sense of a metaphor requires that the reader recognize the potential of similarity within the context of difference and choose which aspect(s) of a relationship between unlike things to interpret in relationship. Metaphors are not simply elements of style, a sort of artistic decoration that embellishes the point that a writer is trying to make. Rather, metaphors stake profound claims about knowing and being, and they encourage us as readers to participate in those claims. Metaphors structure the ways in which we perceive the world. They invite us to understand that categories and prescribed ways of being can be deepened or reformulated to get at meaning that is more than the literal meaning of the terms that metaphors employ. Metaphors render a truth in complex ways that cause us to pause, reflect, and struggle with what is apparently disjunctive in order to see what is new. Metaphors thus create coherence where there was dissimilarity; in this, metaphors are both visionary

14. My electronic forum for Bible study, Ecclesia, has been online since 2006. All are welcome; we have members from across the United States. To join, just go to http://mailman.yale.edu/mailman/listinfo/ecclesia and subscribe.

and transgressive. Metaphors invite us to see with a wider scope and truer depth perception.

In the words of Karsten Harries, "Metaphors speak of what remains absent. All metaphor that is more than an abbreviation for more-proper speech gestures toward what transcends language."[15] Metaphors help to speak new imaginative worlds into being. They not only name things "as they are"; they also invite the reader to perceive the intimate connections between unlike things and the dissimilarities that keep those things from being, in fact, identical. Think of the learning process as you have experienced it in the seminary or college classroom. Now, here are two possible metaphors for your teachers' roles in the mediation of knowledge and skills and insight within the classroom: "gatekeeper" and "midwife." Have you ever had a professor who seemed to function as a gatekeeper, who seemed to see her job as being to guard the purity or intellectual standards of her discipline from poorly articulated theories and shoddy writing? Simply naming that role through the metaphor "gatekeeper" can help you to understand why she did not seem to be primarily engaged in fostering your learning so much as pointing out your mistakes and correcting, or outright rejecting, your novice attempts to enter into the discourse of her field. Have you ever had a professor, conversely, who seemed to function as a midwife, who seemed to see his job as nurturing your tentative insights, fostering your acquisition of needed skills and capacities, and finding something to affirm in your efforts even when he was redirecting your analysis or challenging your writing? Naming that with the metaphor of "midwife" can help you to understand why you felt, even in the hardest labor of the semester, that the professor was an expert companion right there with you, rather than a judge waiting to issue a verdict from on high.

Metaphors matter for how we understand our lives, God, and Scripture. Consider this marvelous story shared by William P. Brown, a professor of Old Testament and ordained minister of Word and Sacrament in the Presbyterian Church (U.S.A.):

> Ten years ago at a small adult Sunday school class, the topic for discussion was how God works in and through people. Near the end of the hour Curtis, a disabled African American Vietnam vet who had suffered a stroke, stood up with some difficulty and delivered what amounted to a conversation stopper: "God's not a microwave, but a Crock-Pot." Without expounding on the remark, he sat down, and a moment of rapt silence ensued, followed by some chuckles and affirmations of agreement. As an eyewitness to this event, I found myself captivated not only by what the speaker meant but also by the

15. Karsten Harries, "Metaphor and Transcendence," in *On Metaphor*, ed. Sheldon Sacks (Chicago: University of Chicago Press, 1979), 82.

> moment of silence that followed as the metaphors worked their magic to prompt reflection.[16]

God is a "Crock-Pot." Hmmm. Let me pause to explain to my younger readers that the Crock-Pot is a slow-cooker that became very popular in the 1970s in the North American suburbs as women began to enter the workforce in greater numbers and thus could not be home to spend hours preparing the evening meal. Now: what does that slow-cooking metaphor suggest to you about the experience of reading Scripture faithfully, or attending church, or understanding the doctrine of the Trinity? Perhaps we are simmering on low heat, as it were, while God works to transform our hearts and minds in subtle ways over time.

Brown suggests that metaphors function much as icons do, presenting us with complex images that may be meditated upon and "read" as icons are read—that's the verb that folks use who are experienced in interpreting iconography. He rightly notes that metaphors "create conceptual and emotional friction by which new meaning is created and the impossible becomes conceivable. . . . It is the metaphor's nature to arrest the hearer and to generate enough lexical ambiguity to provoke the reader's imagination into making associations beneath and beyond its semantic surface."[17] Or in the words of Richard Shiff, metaphor is "a bridge enabling passage from one world to another."[18] Careful and sustained attention to metaphorical language in Scripture, then—and not just to the content, but also to the ways in which metaphorical signifying performs its truths—is necessary if we are to understand Scripture's images and subtle conceptual claims.

Irony

Those who have reflected on haiku or the structure of a symphony know well that silence is as much a part of communication as what is said or otherwise performed. Indeed, what is not said can sometimes be more important than what is said. In some instances, silence in a narrative may signal that whatever is not discussed is simply not in the foreground of the writer's concerns. But in other cases, silence can be thunderously significant. Silences can be playful, opaque, inviting, coercive, secretive, peaceful—the possibilities are endless. Through silence, a writer may be suggesting that something ought not to be said, or is too powerful to be uttered in the wrong company, or

16. William P. Brown, *Seeing the Psalms: A Theology of Metaphor* (Louisville, KY: Westminster John Knox Press, 2002), ix.

17. Ibid., 7–8.

18. Richard Shiff, "Art and Life: A Metaphoric Relationship," in *On Metaphor*, ed. Sheldon Sacks (Chicago: University of Chicago Press, 1979), 106.

cannot be adequately expressed with words, or can only be gestured toward by poetic metaphors fraught with ellipsis. Silence can indicate a focus elsewhere, or it can compel the reader's attention with all the power of an urgent whisper in a crowded room. It is a challenge and a joy for the interpreter to learn, over years of study and reflection, how to listen well to the silences in literature.

Irony is a particularly deft means of signaling through the use of silence. Something is said, certainly, but that "said" is unreliable. The surface meaning in an ironic communication is precisely what is *not* to be trusted. It is by definition inadequate, misleading, only partially true or true in a way that is unimportant compared to more-profound or more-urgent concerns. Whatever is being affirmed—and this is usually something fairly complex—is affirmed tacitly, through cues that show how other understandings or other priorities are false or unworthy. Irony functions by inviting the audience to create meaning within a complex dialogical engagement between the "said" and the "unsaid." This dialogue urges the interpreter into a landscape in which the only visible landmarks are unreliable, and indeed the whole act of communication itself is rendered unstable—yet the reader must nevertheless continue the journey of interpretation.

At the risk of incurring some eye-rolling from those who do not like literary-theory terms, I would like to share my own working definition of irony:

> Irony is a performance of misdirection that generates aporetic interactions between an unreliable "said" and a truer "unsaid" so as to persuade us of something that is subtler, more complex, or more profound than the apparent meaning. Irony disrupts cultural assumptions about the narrative coherence that seems to ground tropological and epistemological transactions, inviting us into an experience of alterity that moves us toward new insight by problematizing false understandings.[19]

Let me translate that a little. Irony undercuts our confidence that we may rely on tropes (such as metaphors or allusions) and straightforward ways of knowing in the interpretive process. We can't trust what we are being told, but nonetheless there is an urgency to the communication. What do we do? How do we respond? Irony is both inviting and unsettling. When we are destabilized as we try to make sense of an ironic text, we find ourselves in a place of irresolvable contradiction that pushes us toward a subtler or more complex "unspoken" truth. Meaning becomes a compelling but elusive "Other" that beckons from beyond the limitations of the "said." False understandings are

19. This definition was first published in my *Irony and Meaning in the Hebrew Bible* (Bloomington: Indiana University Press, 2009), 24.

cut away. We are compelled to grope toward something truer or, at the least, something less vulnerable to being rejected or ironized in turn.

Since the time of the ancient Greeks, philosophers of language have worried that irony might be inherently immoral, given its superficial similarity to lying and dissembling. There is a rich discussion on this in the vast literature on irony, for those who want to pursue it further. For now, I would say that irony is a sophisticated, elegant, and profoundly truthful way of moving beyond the limitations of referential and propositional language. As such, irony is a wonderful gift of God, in Scripture and in life. The faithful reader may delight in the ironies of tone, characterization, plot ("dramatic irony"), and larger literary structure that we can discern in a wide variety of biblical texts. The real risk is to miss the ironies, to read "straight" what was intended to be read in another way. Analysis of irony offers treasures for the attentive interpreter in many parts of the biblical canon, from the Garden of Eden story to the prophecies of Amos, from intercalation in the Gospel of Mark—whereby the writer "sandwiches" one story inside another to ironic effect—to the ironic discourses of Jesus in the Gospel of John.

RECONFIGURING OUR NOTIONS OF HISTORY, TEXT, AND AUTHOR

Every piece of writing springs from the fruitful collision of convictions and imagination. Every act of reading, too, springs from these things: from convictions about the nature of language and text, prior ideas—whether accurate or not—about the subject matter, and readerly imagination about the concepts and cultural landscape in which a particular reading might make sense or be important. As ideological criticism insists, intelligent analysis will always pose the question of whose political or cultural interests the story may be serving in its original context (if one wants to try to figure that out) and/or whose interests are being served by a particular interpretation of the story that is being offered.

Does it matter that different reading strategies yield different results? Is this not all simply the exuberant play of varied perspectives, something that makes the experience of reading in community, and reading across communities, delightfully rich and interesting? Yes and no. Texts may be indeterminate: their meaning cannot be fixed or constrained, but rather is produced through the endless interplay of competing interpretations in a vast, nigh boundless cultural space. Historical critics, too, would readily admit that the evidence is often patient of more than one construal. So we may respond "yes" to the proposal of textual indeterminacy and the play of many readings. But also no: the play of varied perspectives is not simply liberating and interesting, with boundless indeterminacy yielding idiosyncratic provisional readings, each of which can make no lasting claim on any except those who already assent to it. Despite the disclaimers of interpreters these days that theirs is just "one possible" reading or a "provisional" reading that responds to particular needs within their reading location, I have yet to encounter an interpreter who does not indicate (whether overtly or in subtle terms veiled by psychological denial) that his or her own reading should be attended to by others, that his or her reading should matter for others. And some postmodernist interpreters who insist on the constructedness of all reading nevertheless can sometimes be seen to insist on the value of their own interpretations over against others with a rigidity that, in its own peculiar way, rivals that of the older historical critics who pronounce with such certainty on textual issues. Thus the rhetoric of free play and indeterminacy can sometimes be belied by its actual performance in postmodern readings—not always, to be sure, but often enough to be worth remarking as a bona fide contradiction that postmodernists do not generally acknowledge.

> "Post-structuralists usually want to have their cake and eat it. When they are on home ground, they emphasize the playful ('ludic') quality of their interpretations. But as soon as anyone attacks them, they begin to claim some sort of political or moral high ground, and to accuse their opponents of having a repressive view of literature and culture in general—and so of being, in effect, mistaken, even wicked and corrupt, not words that one would expect to belong to the post-structuralist vocabulary."
>
> —John Barton, *Reading the Old Testament* (1996), 222

So what is at stake, when even those who say that there is no one "true" or "best" reading of a text nevertheless imply that some are more worthy of attention than others, relying on the suggested integrity of their own authorial voice even as they insist that "author" is merely a constructed category? Here we arrive again at the notion of witness. The clash of different readings may be heard as Babel, to be sure—as incomprehensibility. But I prefer to hear it as something like the rich cacophony of a music department at a large university. Listen with me: the strains of a Bach cello suite, a violin cadenza from a Vivaldi piece, and mezzo-soprano scales tell us that some musicians are training alone in practice rooms; an African drumming group contributes a stirring, rhythmic beat from upstairs; a chamber choir is rehearsing Palestrina down the hall; dissonances signal that a professor is playing a CD of Schönberg for her music appreciation class; the faint blended chords of a male a cappella group singing "The Whiffenpoof Song" on the street outside are interrupted by a few bars of k. d. lang's "Hallelujah," the ring tone on a student's cell phone. Here are many different dictions, different purposes to performance, and different levels of proficiency in the musicians themselves; some pieces are already polyphonic in their composition, while others become polyphonic only in the experience of the listener; various performers are revealing—whether on purpose or unwittingly—their musicological commitments and idiosyncratic "takes" on style and musicianship; some styles of music dominate, and others are not played that day or perhaps ever in that location (no Javanese gamelan, because the university doesn't have the resources to buy another exotic instrument; no gospel music, because no students have been admitted in recent years who want to study works in that tradition; no Mendelssohn, because the chair of the department gets far too much Mendelssohn at his local church already).

The sounds are beautiful and overwhelming—and they invite us into a lifetime of listening and performing and studying music. Some of us will focus with laser-like intensity on technical problems in musical notation in the medieval period; others will avidly explore musical idioms and musicological issues from as many time periods as they possibly can. So too with the interpretation of Scripture: every approach has value in one or another framework, skill and politics and tradition intermingle, some approaches ignore the theoretical underpinnings of other approaches . . . and the subject being studied cannot be fully understood without the glorious contributions of all.

Finally, we turn to two twentieth-century philosophers whose work can serve as a resource for us to engage literary, ideological, and postmodern aspects of interpretation in a way that honors history. Issues of difference and truth lie at the heart of the historical-critical endeavor. Julia Kristeva and Emmanuel Lévinas have thought well about difference and truth in literature and in the politics of engagement in real communities. Both of them see that ethical principles are at stake in the ways in which we confront those in the past and present who are different from us. Their guidance here will help to equip us for historical-critical and literary-theoretical work that does not remain simplistic, narcissistic, or unengaged.

JULIA KRISTEVA: INTERTEXTUALITY AND FOREIGNNESS

Born in Bulgaria in 1941, Kristeva trained first in philosophy and, later, in psychoanalysis. She moved to Paris at Christmas 1965 when she was twenty-five years old and became established as an important voice in literary analysis, the intersections of language and psychoanalysis, and cultural theory.[20] Two aspects of Kristeva's work will be considered here as important for reading the Bible: her notion of intertextuality and her exploration of foreignness.

Kristeva is credited with having coined the word "intertextuality" in 1966. She named as "intertextuality" the relationships of connection, influence, and meaning that exist culturally among all texts, including this text that I am writing right now and the text—only ostensibly "the same"—that you are reading right now, too. Texts are generated in constant and virtually infinite conversation with other prior texts and are received (in the mind of the interpreter) in relation to subsequent texts in reception history. Texts are intelligible only to the extent that they can be construed to participate in the cultural codes of a particular reader or reading community. Texts are always interpreted according to linguistic and cultural norms—even if those norms remain completely unspoken and, all too often, might be neither understood nor examined by those who are being influenced by them.

Consider this example from early church history. Augustine experienced the joy of full conversion to obedience to God when he picked up a Bible and read Romans 13:13–14: "Let us live . . . not in reveling and drunkenness, not in debauchery and licentiousness, not in quarreling and jealousy. Instead, put on the Lord Jesus Christ, and make no provision for the flesh, to gratify its desires." The book in which Augustine recounts that tale of conversion, his marvelous *Confessions*, has had a huge impact on Christian teaching and the Western cultural heritage more generally, particularly as regards Augustine's groundbreaking use of spiritual autobiography and his conflicted view of human sexuality. The text from Romans 13 that we now read in our Bibles is not "the same" text that Augustine read some sixteen hundred years ago. It has forever been changed by our knowledge of Augustine's having being convicted by it and by all the refractions of text and Augustine and responses to Augustine that churches and cultures have generated. Further, today Romans 13 is read privately, studied in scholarly articles, and proclaimed in worship in the churches in cultural worlds that are far different from the world that shaped Augustine, so influences from other directions, as well, make it a different text than it could have been in the first centuries of the early church.

Intertextuality has been variously described as a mosaic, a matrix, or a web of allusive relationships. Whatever metaphor we choose, the idea of intertextuality suggests that no text or utterance may rightly be interpreted as if it had emerged in a vacuum. Every text's claims are already complicated, contested, affirmed, elaborated, and reframed in an infinite variety of ways in

20. Julia Kristeva's official Web site, http://www.kristeva.fr/, makes available a number of her texts in English and French. Another prominent figure in the development of ideas about intertextuality is French literary critic and philosopher Roland Barthes.

relationship to other texts and utterances. We could spend wonderfully productive time thinking about inner-biblical allusions, cross-cultural influences, relationships of literary dependence between and among biblical texts, and the rich generativity of new intertextualities in the reception history of Scripture: the countless ways in which Scripture verses, images, characters, ideas, and tropes have been taken up and responded to in art, music, literature, theology, and wider culture. For our purposes here, I encourage you to allow the notion of intertextuality to deepen your appreciation of the richly layered and complex ways in which biblical texts signify their truths and are received, both by you as a reader today and by communities of faith from ancient days to the present. There is never one monolithic meaning to be gleaned from any single text, much less from a diverse corpus within Scripture (such as the Primeval History, the Deuteronomistic History, or the Pauline Epistles) or from Scripture taken as a whole.

Does this mean that "any interpretation goes"? Not to me, although each reader will have her or his own answer to that question. I consider myself to be a faithful Christian reader because I read in conversation with the whole canon of Scripture, I read always in intentional relationship to my baptism and my confessional affirmation of the unique revelation of God in Jesus Christ, and I read in dialogue with many different traditions of Christian interpretation, from patristic readings to medieval mystics' reflections to Luther's exegesis to contemporary Anglican theology. Also essential, for me, is a posture of eagerness for and openness to the work of the Holy Spirit when I read, whether I am in my office or in a worship service. For me, analyzing Scripture and studying diverse responses to Scripture—from Augustine's conversion experience to a poem by Mark Doty to the latest article on biblical historiography in the *Journal of Biblical Literature*—are acts of Christian devotion no less than prayer and worship are, because the ultimate purpose of my study is to help me to understand God better and praise God more fully.

Multiple ways of reading Scripture, then, need not be seen as a threat to faithful reading. They may be construed as a wondrous gift: different avenues toward faithfulness suited to different interpretive and spiritual journeys, all of which may be superintended by the Holy Spirit. No avenue of interpretation, no matter what its foundational hermeneutical assumptions, can possibly resist the grace of God working through the Holy Spirit. I know well that some ecclesial traditions frame things differently. That's fine. I share my own posture toward faithful reading simply to invite you to consider your own commitments and convictions about how you may engage the Word as you learn about different methodological approaches.

Back to Kristeva. She offers some provocative thoughts about foreignness that are useful when we consider different ways of reading Scripture.

Foreignness as a trope—as a metaphor and motif, not just as a literal descriptor for origin from another place—is central to Kristeva's thought. She has reflected on the conflicts generated in French culture around experiences of ethnic foreignness, including her own experience as a Bulgarian who has made France her home. Kristeva wrestles in her work with the pressures that a dominant culture places on those who are Other, and we may extrapolate from her thought as we consider biblical hermeneutics. For it is not just people who are construed as outsiders by social systems or who feel themselves to be "foreign" to the environments in which they live. Texts and other cultural expressions continually trade on, reveal anxiety about, or exploit difference as well. And the "difference" of foreignness is not only something that is experienced from outside the subjectivity of a person. As a psychoanalyst, Kristeva has insight into the kinds of "foreignness" that are repressed or expressed within the human psyche as well. As anyone knows who has engaged in psychotherapy, dream work, spiritual direction, vocational discernment, addiction recovery work, or another means of coming to know oneself more fully, there are dimensions and parts of ourselves that we would prefer not to acknowledge, or that even may come as a complete surprise when they are brought to the attention of our conscious mind. Kristeva writes about multiple or fractured subjectivities in the realms of the psyche and culture:

> Psychoanalysis makes us admit "I is an other" and even several others. . . . If God becomes a stable Value, if the Person coheres into a stable identity, all well and good, but all the energy of modern culture is directed against this homogeneity and tendency toward stagnation—what it exposes instead is fragmentation. Not only are we divided, harboring within "ourselves" alterities we can sometimes hardly bear, but this polyphony gives us pleasure.[21]

There are ethical implications to be mined here in terms of the cultures in which we live as readers and the ways in which we view "foreignness" within Scripture. Kristeva continues, "By recognizing this strangeness intrinsic to each of us, we have more opportunities to tolerate the foreignness of others. And subsequently more opportunities to try to create less monolithic, more polyphonic communities."[22]

Extrapolating to the realm of hermeneutics, we may reflect on ways in which Scripture texts harbor within themselves traces of "foreignness" that would be a surprise to whatever dominant discourse controls the most prevalent or loudest or most obvious features of signifying in that text. This

21. Julia Kristeva, *Revolt, She Said: An Interview by Philippe Petit*, trans. Brian O'Keeffe (Los Angeles: Semiotext[e], 2002), 63–64.

22. Ibid., 64.

question is related to deconstruction: a literary-critical and philosophical means of engagement that seeks to unravel or destabilize a discourse's official "performance" by drawing attention to irreducible conflicts, vulnerabilities, and contradictions within that discourse's own logic. Even harsh polemics or apparently ironclad ideologies suppress within themselves the traces of what they are trying to obliterate. We might consider here the stubborn presence of Rahab in the discourse of conquest-obsessed Joshua. As a Canaanite female prostitute, Rahab represents a triple threat to the boundaries of the "social body" of Israel. She is an autonomous woman, and thus anomalous, dangerous, and in need of being controlled by males per the essentialist patriarchalism of ancient Israelite society; and she is both a prostitute and a Canaanite, which represents sexual threat twice over for a stream of tradition in which sexual mixing with foreigners yields death (see Num. 25).[23] Rahab is dangerous, all right—but she has been written ineradicably into the midst of Israel (Josh. 6:25). We might also consider the Moabite lineage of the glorious King David (see Ruth 4:13–22) in light of the uncompromising Deuteronomic ban on the presence of Moabites in the Israelite worshiping assembly (Deut. 23:3–4). These are only two of many examples that could be mustered within the Hebrew Scriptures of narratives and poems and legal material that bear within themselves "gaps" or "loose threads" or moments of conflict that can be probed by the faithful interpreter.

> "While in the most savage human groups the foreigner was an enemy to be destroyed, he has become, within the scope of religious and ethical constructs, a different human being who, provided he espouses them, may be assimilated into the fraternities of the 'wise,' the 'just,' or the 'native.'"
>
> —Julia Kristeva, "Toccata and Fugue for the Foreigner,"
> in *Strangers to Ourselves* (1991), 2

The psychological, social, and cultural pressures to assimilate—to hide foreignness—are strong indeed. But Kristeva's work encourages us to see the recognition and embrace of foreignness as an opportunity. Consider the varied pressures of ancient Israelite social and theological norms expressed in Scripture texts, the pressures of your own ecclesial tradition, and the pressures of the academy (in your seminary classroom, or, if you are a pastor, in the MDiv curriculum back when you were taking courses). Can you name

23. For an interpretation of the risk that Rahab represents to Israelite holy-war discourse, see my "The Formation of Godly Community: Old Testament Hermeneutics in the Presence of the Other," *Anglican Theological Review* 86 (2004): 623–36.

those pressures? Can you see the ways in which you have been seduced into trusting that you will be considered wise and righteous if only you will bow to this or that way of thinking? I invite you to be alert to these pressures and to engage them intentionally, honoring your own "foreignness" as a reader and interpreter wherever you might be tempted to assimilate and lose what makes you uniquely yourself.

We should remember that historical criticism itself is a powerful tool for helping us to listen to and honor foreignness. The Hebrew Scriptures brim with the testimonies of people and communities that were vastly different from the modern contexts in which we live. Historical criticism seeks to hear the differences between who we are, contextually, and the lived contexts of ancient peoples. Sophisticated historical inquiry is an indispensable tool for the Christian, if it be plied as a provisional but committed attentiveness to the plural testimonies of witnesses to an incarnational God.

Let's turn to our focus text, Judges 4–5. How might Kristeva's ruminations on intertextuality and foreignness help us to read the story of Jael and Sisera? We might read the story as a response to holy-war texts in the ancient Near Eastern milieu. Interpreted as a response to that environment, the story may be seen to demonstrate the ancient Canaanite culture's higher level of toleration for the figure of the woman warrior. Why? The ethnic identity of Jael is never stated in the biblical text, but given the text's self-consciousness about Jael being married to a Kenite, it would be plausible to assume that she is understood in the story as a Canaanite woman. Thus she may be constructed as a "foreigner." We also know that the warrior-goddess Anat was a major figure in the Canaanite pantheon.[24] Stories tell of Anat's battles with other deities; she is hymned for her victories in vivid terms that describe her wading knee-deep in the blood of those she has slain. Jael's military power in dispatching the top enemy commander singlehandedly draws on the cultural intertext of foreign (Canaanite) mythology, channeling that power into an Israelite story that responds, in the larger intertextual universe, to Israelite holy war traditions. Thus the figure of the lone and vulnerable Jael may hide the silhouette of the ferocious Anat with her bloody sword.

Reading intertextually, we may locate Jael in a literary landscape that includes other women warriors in ancient Hebrew tradition, including Esther and Judith. There the warrior-heroines are clearly portrayed as faithful to their people and their Jewish heritage (although with Esther, her initial anxieties about revealing her Jewish identity, combined with her utter lack of concern about sexual congress with a foreign male and failing to keep kosher,

24. For a guide to ancient texts featuring Anat, see Bill T. Arnold and Bryan E. Beyer, eds., *Readings from the Ancient Near East: Primary Sources for Old Testament Study* (Grand Rapids: Baker Academic, 2002).

render her a complicated heroine in terms of her Jewishness). Here in Judges 4–5, Jael is a foreigner through and through. We might interpret that ironically: the cultural interaction between Canaanite and Israelite traditions serves to feminize Israel's traditions of mighty men of valor and to introduce foreignness into the very heart of Israelite identity. Jael has won more than one battle here. Her valor has defeated not only Sisera but also the rigidity of ancient Israelite traditions that proscribe intermarriage with Canaanite women (as Deuteronomistic tradition does). The figure of Jael, beckoning at the entrance of her tent, may evoke not only the woman warrior but also the figure of the Strange Woman from Proverbs 7. She lures in the wayward male who cannot see, through the fog of seductive possibility, that to go to her will "cost him his life" (Prov. 7:23). In this, Jael may stand as an icon for all that threatens Israelite wisdom and cultural integrity. Yet foreignness—Jael's gendered and ethnic Otherness—has shamed Israelite power no less than Canaanite power. Barak's ineffectual whining about needing Deborah's presence is shown up for the cowardice it is by Jael's quiet display of deadly force alone in her tent. Israel's implicit dependence here on foreign resources is left as a problematic trace over which later Israelite traditions, including prophetic traditions, will worry.

EMMANUEL LÉVINAS: THE FACE OF THE OTHER AND THE INTERRUPTION OF DISCOURSE

Emmanuel Lévinas was born in Lithuania in 1906. His family was Jewish, and his lifelong connection to Judaism was evident in his essays on Judaism and, later in life, work on talmudic texts. He studied in Freiburg and became a philosopher of phenomenology, which is a branch of philosophy that focuses on consciousness and its correlates, such as perspective, memory, and imagination. Lévinas was appointed to positions at various French universities. His last appointment was at the Sorbonne starting in 1973; he died in 1995. His writings focus on philosophy and ethics.[25] Two related ideas of Lévinas that I find fruitful for biblical hermeneutics have to do with his notion of attending to the Other and his suggestion that interrupting discourse is an ethical imperative.

A fundamental point of Lévinas's ethical philosophy is the idea that we are required, by ethics and by truth, to be present to the face of the Other with

25. A Lévinas Web site is maintained by Peter Atterton, a professor of philosophy at San Diego State University: http://www.levinas.sdsu.edu/index.htm. The Stanford Encyclopedia of Philosophy offers a substantive assessment of Lévinas's work: http://plato.stanford.edu/entries/levinas/.

as much integrity and compassion as we can, rather than to use the Other for our own purposes. The Other is the one who is different from us, the one whose desires and needs are other than ours and may conflict with ours. We may construct that difference according to various characteristics: the racially or ethnically distinct Other, the Other whose gender or sexual identity is not expressed in the way we express our own, the Other whose cultural norms or educational background or social needs present a "problem" for our view of the world. But ultimately, the face of the Other is prior to any way we have of understanding who that Other is. And the Other makes an absolute ethical claim on us. Lévinas writes,

> To speak, at the same time as knowing the Other, is making oneself known to him. The Other is not only known, he is *greeted* [*salué*]. He is not only named, but also invoked. To put it in grammatical terms, the Other does not appear in the nominative, but in the vocative. I not only think of what he is for me, but also and simultaneously, and even before, I *am* for him.[26]

In one of his most poignant formulations, Lévinas says that the ethical mandate for every human being is "not to let the other die alone."[27] Whenever we are tempted to privilege one kind of biblical discourse and ignore another, or when we are eager to use one ancient witness to "trump" another in our ecclesial debates, we would do well to remember the powerful theological implications of the Lévinasian mandate "not to let the other die alone."

> "The neighbor concerns me before all assumption, all commitment consented to or refused. I am bound to him. . . . He orders me before being recognized. . . . The face of a neighbor signifies for me an unexceptionable responsibility, preceding every free consent, every pact, every contract."
>
> —Emmanuel Lévinas, *Otherwise Than Being, Or Beyond Essence*, trans. Alphonso Lingis (1974), 87–88

Lévinas argues that the Otherness of the neighbor is an interruption of totalizing discourse. What does that mean? Well, "totalizing" is a negative term; in ethical and philosophical thought, it tends to carry a negative sense of being coercive and aggressively universalistic in a way that is actually false or even violent to local idiosyncrasies or particularities. As Tamara Cohn

26. Emmanuel Lévinas, *Difficult Freedom: Essays on Judaism* (London: Athlone Press, 1990), 7.

27. Emmanuel Lévinas, *Alterity and Transcendence*, trans. Michael B. Smith (New York: Columbia University Press, 1999), 29.

Eskenazi says, "Totality dehumanizes by erasing the particular."[28] In this context, then, "interruption" connotes an ethically valuable disruption of a purportedly universal claim, narrative, or framework that is doing harm. All narratives and systems of thought explain things and try to communicate the truth of things by suggesting that particular stories, subjects, doctrines, laws, or causes are coherent and meaningful. The problem comes, inevitably, because systems of explanation leave things out and distort things. Cultural discourses cannot avoid marginalizing and misrepresenting things, even with the best of intentions of all concerned. So "interruption" of the ways that we marginalize and misrepresent may be understood as revolutionary (in a good way) or, to put it in theological terms, as a prophetic intervention that speaks truth to power.

The Lévinasian valorization of the interruption of totalizing discourse has profound implications for biblical interpretation. Not every biblical discourse need be construed as "totalizing," although in every case, assessment of that will be in the eye of the reader. I would argue that ironic biblical texts make space for alternative readings because their meaning lies in an unspoken that is beyond "the said." I think that the elliptical nature of poetic expression in the Psalms invites multiple constructions of the "gaps" there and, as a consequence, multiple experiences of truth. I would maintain that the complexity of certain characters in biblical narrative—such as Joseph, Saul, Job, and Qohelet—empowers the reader to entertain divergent assessments of the rhetorics proclaimed by those characters. But some types of discourse in the Bible certainly do lay down their own perspective as definitive and impervious to objection. And in some cases, biblical discourses encode within their own narratives the idea that the penalty for resistance to their norms is actual death. (Consider the deadly aftermath of the Golden Calf incident in Exodus 32; consider what holy-war discourse is suggesting in the story of Achan; reflect on what it might mean that pentateuchal legal materials prescribe the death penalty for certain religious or social offenses.) According to the philosophical program of Lévinas, it is an ethical imperative for us to interrupt scriptural discourse that coerces in a way that is destructive to the experience of others.

Now, Scripture also champions the cause of the orphan, the widow, the sojourner, and the poor, and some texts allow for competing claims to remain unresolved—there is plenty of ground on which we can stake a claim for liberatory and nontotalizing discourses within the Bible. But our appropriation of biblical texts may be ethically complicated even when the Scripture story in question seems to be one of liberation and grace. Consider the story of the

28. Tamara Cohn Eskenazi, "Introduction—Facing the Text as Other: Some Implications of Levinas's Work for Biblical Studies," in *Levinas and Biblical Studies*, ed. Tamara Cohn Eskenazi, Gary A. Phillips, and David Jobling (Atlanta: Society of Biblical Literature, 2003), 6.

exodus. The tradition that God brought the Israelites out of slavery in Egypt is foundational for ancient Israelite understandings of God as redeemer. It has become the paradigmatic story of deliverance in Jewish tradition, and reflections on the exodus—both as historical event and as metaphor—lie at the heart of Christian theological traditions about God's saving work in Jesus Christ. But the exodus story has a dark side that poses serious ethical problems: it required the wholesale slaughter of many Egyptians, and not only the pursuing Egyptian military but also innocent firstborn Egyptian boys and youth throughout the land. John J. Collins names this and other ethical difficulties in biblical texts with admirable candor:

> The episode of the plagues shows that Exodus is not only the story of the liberation of Israel, but also the story of the defeat and humiliation of the Egyptians. The latter aspect of the story involves nationalistic, ethnic vengeance, which is less than edifying. The plagues affect not only Pharaoh and the taskmasters, but also, even especially, the common Egyptians, who also labored under Pharaoh. The most chilling plague is the slaughter of the firstborn. . . . The demand for the death of the firstborn bespeaks the hungry God, whom we have already encountered in Genesis 22 [in the story of the near-sacrifice of Isaac]. . . . At least Exodus appreciates the depth of grief to which this gives rise, but in the end there is little sympathy for the Egyptians.[29]

While we may read a subtle sympathy for the Egyptian Other between the lines of the stories about Hagar in Genesis 16 and 21, I would argue that there is no real compassion at all for the faceless Egyptians in the book of Exodus. In most biblical rhetoric, the Egyptian constitutes a hated enemy. In the prophetic corpus we see intense interest in warning Israel not to rely on Egypt—that is, not to turn to an alliance with Egypt in an attempt to save themselves from some other military threat, such as Assyria or Babylon (see Isa. 30:1–7; 31:1–3; Jer. 46:1–24; Ezek. 29:1–16).

The ethical work of Lévinas is helpful when we reread the story of Jael and Sisera again. Who is constituted as "Other" by the narrative strategies of this story, and what are the possibilities for interruption of coercive discourse here? That latter question has two aspects: (1) Is the narrator performing an interruption of Israelite cultural discourse of his own? (2) May we interrupt what the narrator is doing as well, from our own ethical position outside of his cultural world?

A feminist reading could make the case that Jael, as Canaanite and as woman, is the Other in a patriarchal story world. There is merit to that position. But I prefer to consider the actual enemy, the one whose intrusion into

29. John J. Collins, *Introduction to the Hebrew Bible* (Minneapolis: Fortress Press, 2004), 113.

the community is met with dehumanizing violence: Sisera. For the ancient Israelite narrator and for contemporary readers who do not resist the narrator's framing of things, Sisera may be the face of the Other in this story. How could he be otherwise? He is commodified as a hostile force to be overcome in order for Israel's narrative of triumph to continue.

The narrator underlines Sisera's power and indomitability. This Canaanite military leader commands nine hundred chariots of iron, likely an inflated number for a small tribal group centered around the village of Hazor. If historical-critical work demonstrates that this number of chariots has likely been significantly inflated, we may postulate that an ideological purpose is at work here to give the impression of overwhelming force against which the plucky Israelites fight valiantly. This commander "oppressed the Israelites ruthlessly for twenty years" (Judg. 4:3; while one might expect the accountability for the oppression to lie with King Jabin, "Sisera" lies closer to hand as the syntactical antecedent). The Hebrew there underlines the relentless pressure of Sisera's forces on the Israelites. The verb can mean either "press" or "oppress," and it is worth noting that it is used in Judges 1—in a narrative of Israel's military aggression and strength against the indigenous Canaanites—to describe the way in which the Amorites "pressed" the tribe of Dan into the hill country; hence, it need not necessarily connote brutal oppression on the part of Jabin and Sisera. Many Canaanite groups had fought against Israel during the period of the judges (see Judg. 2), "pressing" and "crowding" the Israelites, which means, at the least, not yielding their territory to the Israelite invaders gracefully. Here in the story of Jael and Sisera, we see an interest in underlining the power of Sisera. His army is portrayed as invincible: as with the Egyptians in the exodus story, so too this story gives us an implacable enemy whose only role in the narrative is to serve as an object of hate and resistance.

In Deuteronomistic holy-war ideology, God fights against Israel's enemies, routing them with a supernatural panic. So it goes here: Israel gains the upper hand and pursues the fleeing Canaanites relentlessly, cutting down every last enemy soldier. Sisera escapes on foot, fleeing to territory he considers safe: the tent of an ally. Jael is alone in the tent. On her own initiative, she goes out to meet him and invites him in. Pause with me to picture this. Since Sisera had to abandon his chariot and flee on foot, we may imagine that he had been surrounded by Israelites in the thick of battle such that his chariot could not move; perhaps his horse had been slain. This is not a military man in dress whites striding toward Jael's tent—we may picture a gasping, exhausted, terrified man staggering toward her, covered in blood, the sole survivor of a military massacre of his men. He whispers, with respect (the Hebrew there is polite and self-effacing), his request for a little water and for sanctuary.

Jael offers words of reassurance and a bowl of milk. And then she butchers him as he sleeps. Mighty Jael, whose exploit will be immortalized in the war songs of her enemies! By this act, Jael has atoned for the treachery of her husband in aligning himself with the Canaanites over against the people of Moses (possibly relevant here is 1 Sam. 15:6). Sisera is worthy of no pity. Except . . . we may read this story "otherwise." We may read that Sisera was the leader of the indigenous local Canaanite population who had been trying for twenty years to repel rapacious Israelite invaders who had fallen upon the Canaanites unprovoked, as Judges 1 makes clear. Israel had come streaming into Canaan under the banner of holy war, charged by their god to let nothing that breathes remain alive (Deut. 20:16–18). Resistance—pressing Israel to desist from its goal of conquest of Canaanite territory and total annihilation of the Canaanites—is the crime of which Jabin and his trusted army commander are guilty. There is no doubt as to where the sympathies of the biblical narrator lie. Israel is meant to win; the Canaanites are meant to die in a bloodbath. But for the reader who hears Lévinas's call not to commodify the Other, matters may not be so simple. We may read resistantly.

Perhaps Jael is not so convinced of her own heroism as the biblical narrator is. Perhaps she sees, as Rahab did before her, that there is only one viable choice in the face of the overwhelming Israelite victory against the Canaanite forces that were trying to protect her. Perhaps she loathes herself for her betrayal of Sisera, whose troops might have included her own husband, Heber, that very day, now dead. Slaughter begets slaughter. The blood of all the slain runs together. War requires the utter dehumanization of the foe. How else could Jael have assassinated an ally of her husband who had begged for her help, gratefully received her hospitality, and collapsed into sleep, trusting in her protection?

For me, Sisera is the face of the Other. He is despised by the biblical narrator, who shows him no pity, narratologically speaking. But Lévinas's ethic requires that we see as inhuman not the Other, not the foreigner and the enemy, but the violence that dehumanizes all of us. The challenge is twofold when we read the story of Jael and Sisera with Lévinas as our conversation partner. We must look into the face of the slaughtered Sisera and hold him accountable for his actions. But we must look also into the face of Jael, as she wipes Sisera's blood from her hair and tries to avoid our gaze. Jael the heroine, or Jael the murderous traitor? This story is too permeated by violence and loss for us to be satisfied with any triumphalist metanarrative. This story tries to coerce us into reading with the Israelites—of that there is no doubt. And indeed, as we bend over the corpse of Sisera, we may be fearful: for all we know, the narrator's Jael may be stealthily approaching us with another tent peg in her bloodstained hand. But Lévinas asks that we look on Sisera anyway.

An ethic of alterity insists that we gaze at his devastated face and perhaps even speak his name. While the story of Jael and Sisera performs its own "interruption" of the Canaanite threat, we may choose a reading attentive to the Other that insists on an interruption of the holy-war discourse of Joshua and Judges.

The educated biblical interpreter today must wrestle with debates about authorial intention, textual indeterminacy, and reader agency. I hope you find this interpretive work exciting rather than daunting or faithless. Powerful indeed is the notion that we are called to attend to the Other within Scripture and within our own interpretive practices. Christians worship a God who became incarnate in a world of particularities. The Gospels are full of stories about the ways in which our Messiah engaged his people's lived and contested experiences of God. Exploring different approaches to reading Scripture can only illumine the path of faithfulness, if we engage those approaches with integrity and openness to the action of the Holy Spirit.

FOR FURTHER READING

Boer, Roland, ed. *Bakhtin and Genre Theory in Biblical Studies.* Atlanta: Society of Biblical Literature, 2007.

Collins, John J. *The Bible after Babel: Historical Criticism in a Postmodern Age.* Grand Rapids: Wm. B. Eerdmans Pub. Co., 2005.

Davis, Ellen F. *Getting Involved with God: Rediscovering the Old Testament.* Cambridge: Cowley Pubs., 2001.

Eskenazi, Tamara Cohn, Gary A. Phillips, and David Jobling, eds. *Lévinas and Biblical Studies.* Atlanta: Society of Biblical Literature, 2003.

Gillingham, Susan E. *One Bible, Many Voices: Different Approaches to Biblical Studies.* Grand Rapids: Wm. B. Eerdmans Pub. Co., 1998.

Green, Barbara. *Mikhail Bakhtin and Biblical Scholarship: An Introduction.* Atlanta: Society of Biblical Literature, 2000.

Gunn, David M. "Judges 4–5." In *Judges,* 53–92. Blackwell Bible Commentaries. Oxford: Blackwell Pub., 2005.

2

One Truth or Many Voices?

Literary Sources and the Integrity of the Text

It was a sunny October morning at Yale Divinity School. Marquand Chapel was absolutely packed for the 10:30 a.m. worship service. I took one of the few available seats, near the door. A group of seminarians was leading the worship service that morning; we sang a stirring hymn and heard a fine sermon from a student preacher. A student rose to lead the prayers; intercessions and petitions were lifted up on behalf of the gathered community. She began a prayer of thanksgiving for Scripture, and I rejoiced until I heard her offer this: "And we thank you, God, for the beauty of your Holy Word. Help us to continue to cherish it even when they take our Scripture and"—her voice trembled with rising anger—"tear it to pieces in the classroom." Stunned and hurt, I slipped out of the chapel service to reflect on what had just happened. "Our" Scripture was being slashed to pieces by "them"—by the YDS Bible faculty. By me and my colleagues. We were being labeled with the hostile word "them" in this prayer-as-weapon. Rage simmered just below the surface of the student's prayer. She saw biblical scholarship, or at least a certain kind of scholarly inquiry, as profoundly harmful to her faith.

It is possible that the student was enrolled in the big New Testament introductory course and had been struggling with historical-Jesus debates or conflicting traditions in the Gospels. But I was fairly sure she was in the Old Testament introductory course. That class deals with pentateuchal criticism in the fall semester, including lectures on the Documentary Hypothesis. According to that theory, four different written sources are interwoven in Genesis, Exodus, Leviticus, Numbers, and Deuteronomy (and possibly in Joshua and other biblical books; scholars disagree on the extent of the sources). I was not teaching that introductory course this particular semester; we rotate the course among the Old Testament faculty, and one of my colleagues was at the helm this time. But I was shocked by the student's use of prayer publicly to attack critical analysis of the Hebrew Scriptures as if it were obviously antagonistic to the life of faith. Even though I didn't happen to be teaching the class, I felt wounded by her implication that faculty who employ these methods couldn't possibly cherish Scripture. I didn't know the name of the student, so I let it go—a missed opportunity for mutual dialogue and healing, to be sure. The incident took place years ago. If I were to meet the student today, I would say to her: "I'm so sorry that course was challenging for you. I hope someone helped you to process the disruption in your faith that you experienced while learning about source criticism. This chapter is for you."

The church isn't much interested in the Documentary Hypothesis. For many pastors and seminary students, it would seem that the notion of Yahwistic, Elohistic, Priestly, and Deuteronomistic sources in the Pentateuch is an arcane hypothetical idea of no real value to today's believers. Dismissive jokes about J, E, P, and D are the rule in ecclesial circles, if the classic sources are mentioned at all. Denominations that seek to train learned clergy and are open to the results of biblical scholarship, such as my own Episcopal Church, seem to draw the line at critical inquiry more technical than one might encounter in a religious studies class at the introductory college level. In my tradition, technical research is not necessarily considered to be wrong or bad for faith, but it is implicitly treated as irrelevant a lot of the time. A simplified theory about J, E, P, and D is something that most ordained pastors have had to consider at least briefly if they attended seminary in North America in the twentieth century. But the relevance of source criticism for the contemporary life of faith is seldom explored. Source criticism of the Pentateuch yields a type of scholarly result that is often characterized as "fragmentation" of the biblical narrative and either mocked from the pulpit or ignored.

THE YAHWIST DOESN'T HAVE MANY FRIENDS ON FACEBOOK

Shortly before this book went to press, I asked my Facebook friends whether they had ever heard of J, E, P, and D in church, either from the pulpit or in a parish Bible study. Listen to these responses:

> SURE, I did!!! J was for Jesus, E was for Elohim, P was for the Passion (of the Christ), and D was for Die Daily (as in Luke 9:23), LOL. (Lyvonne, a 28-year-old evangelical)

> I taught JEPD to my adult ed classes back in the 1970s. Most people looked at me like there was something terribly wrong with me. (Mary, a 59-year-old Episcopalian who taught in a Roman Catholic context)

> The first time I heard about the Documentary Hypothesis was when I told my pastor I was going to graduate school for theology. At which point he proceeded to give me a crash course: "Here's what they're going to try to tell you about the Bible; here's a stack of books to tell you why they're wrong." I've thought back to that exchange many times over the years, and two things in particular stand out. (1) It seemed blatantly unfair, even at the time, that my pastor had this wealth of "secret" biblical knowledge that he wasn't willing to share with the congregation. Why was I only hearing about this at age twenty-one, and just because I happened to be going to graduate school? (2) I would have had a *much* better experience in graduate biblical studies if someone had introduced me to the basics of source criticism in an ecclesial setting, perhaps starting in high school. (Melanie, a 32-year-old nondenominational evangelical)

Lyvonne's response beautifully—and hilariously—reframes the question, showing that the priorities of her faith community were adamantly christological in focus. Mary's response describes the staunch resistance she encountered at the parish level when she introduced discussion of pentateuchal sources. Melanie's response illustrates the profound antagonism toward scholarly inquiry into Scripture she encountered on the part of a clergy person. (I had a similar experience in college myself. When I decided to go to divinity school, I was thrilled. I told a visiting evangelical speaker, assuming that he would have inspiring words to share about the joys of theological learning that awaited me. I was surprised and disappointed that all he offered was a stern admonition: "Don't let seminary destroy your faith!") Suspicion of critical inquiry clearly exists in plenty of places throughout the church, even when that critical inquiry is performed by deeply devout scholars and students passionate for the gospel. Have you ever noticed that a subtle distinction between "scholars" and believers is often implicit in church-speak? I have never heard a pastor acknowledge from the pulpit that biblical scholars might be singing in the choir that morning, hosting coffee hour, or serving on the pastoral care committee. In my experience, when clergy refer to scholars from the pulpit, they often construct us as disembodied rationalists who are at best indifferent to everything that matters to true believers.

But surely we can agree that Bible readers need guidance in coming to terms with what is confusing or unexpected in our sacred texts. And anyone who reads the flood story closely will notice that discrepancies abound; different versions are preserved. Did one pair of every animal go into the ark, or was it seven pairs? (Cf. Gen. 6:19 and 7:2.) Did the flood waters cover the earth for

40 days or 150 days? (Cf. Gen. 7:17 and 7:24.) The only way *not* to notice those discrepancies is to read without paying attention. Yet the idea that different versions of the same story in a biblical text or markedly different emphases in ancient theological views *already* cause a sense of disjuncture or fragmentation for the alert reader is seldom articulated from the pulpit or in parish Bible studies. It must be frustrating for readers with no training to encounter these problems but never hear anything about how to address them.

WHY SOURCE CRITICISM?

Source critics have labored long and hard to try to demonstrate that in the first five books of the Bible, and particularly visibly in Genesis and Exodus, the alert reader can discern distinct literary sources interwoven and juxtaposed with one another, each with a characteristic diction, theology, and plotline all its own. The so-called Yahwist (J) generated a narrative of creation and patriarchal stories that speak of a God in intimate and evolving relationship with human beings. The J material allows its characters to use the Tetragrammaton name for God, YHWH—translated in English Bibles as "the Lord"—even at points in the plot before that special name has been revealed to Moses at the burning bush (Exod. 3:14). The Priestly writer or school (P) envisions a transcendent God by whose all-powerful hand the cosmos has been ordered and structured. This Priestly God demands appropriate marks of covenantal obedience in the people whom God has chosen; in the Priestly material is an intense focus on circumcision of male believers, rubrics for sacrifice, and other rituals by means of which Israel lives in right relationship with this holy God. The shadowy Elohist (E) has supplied fragments of material or a fuller narrative (it depends on which scholar you ask), characterized by the theological portrayal of God—named as Elohim before the revelation of the Tetragrammaton—as a hidden deity who reveals divine purposes via angels and dreams. This so-called E source uses the name "Horeb" for the mountain that other sources call Sinai. Finally, the Deuteronomic school (D) has supplied a discernible Deuteronomistic stratum of narrative and legal material concerned with the conditional terms of the covenant between God and Israel, blessings and curses, and the reliable fulfillment of prophetic predictions in the political life of Israel and Judah as a trustworthy indicator of God's sovereignty.

Do these literary layers matter for interpretation? Certainly not to everyone. Synchronic readers of many different stripes insist that the final form of a text is the only form of that text that we can study, and pastors seem to enjoy ridiculing the highly technical minutiae of source-critical analysis. To be sure, the interpreter would do well to take account of the final form of the text at some stage in her analysis, whether beginning there as a way to encounter the interplay between coherence and disjuncture or ending there with a fuller understanding of the character and thrust of each of the different layers that supply narrative and theological impetus for the larger text. And it is true that in practice, source critics have tended to divide up the biblical narratives into isolated verses and half-verses as they work hard to imagine what the theoretically distinct narratives could have said before being interwoven. That's a by-product of the method, and it can be annoying to read. Source criticism need not be seen as intrinsically hostile to Scripture: it could just as well be seen as a really careful kind of *listening* to Scripture! But the method does privilege a wholesale disruption of the final literary form in service of a quest for origins that not every reader finds exciting. David Clines, a professor at Sheffield University, shares this anecdote about the priorities of Old Testament study in his institution, which is known for postmodern literary and cultural analysis:

> One of our external examiners for our undergraduate degree, a personage from a famous medieval university, let me note, reproached us in Sheffield a few years ago because our graduating students seemed to have a very hazy notion of the documentary theory of the Pentateuch, or perhaps no notion at all. How could we let students do three years of biblical studies and not be proficient in Pentateuchal origins? "Very easily," we answered; "we were busy doing lots of other things with them, and, in a word, we forgot!" There was no conspiracy to exclude JEDP from the course; it just didn't manage to impose itself sufficiently upon us to ensure its place in the curriculum.[1]

In many other theological learning environments, too, the Documentary Hypothesis is just not considered to be the most important thing to know about the Pentateuch. Nor—despite protestations of historical critics to the contrary—is an extended and highly detailed inquiry into the composition of the Pentateuch a natural or necessary starting place for instruction about the Torah literature.

Yet I am convinced that it is valuable to wrestle with the implications of the theory, even though most days, I have serious doubts about some of the assumptions underlying it. In what follows, we will consider the significance

1. David J. A. Clines, "Response to Rolf Rendtorff," in "What Happened to the Yahwist? Reflections after Thirty Years: A Collegial Conversation between Rolf Rendtorff, David J. A. Clines, Allen Rosengren, and John Van Seters," in *Probing the Frontiers of Biblical Studies*, ed. J. Harold Ellens and John T. Greene (Eugene, OR: Pickwick Pubs., 2009), 51.

of source criticism for a faithful reading of Scripture. Mine will by no means be a comprehensive treatment of the method. As I noted in the introduction, there are many fine books already published about hermeneutical methods, the history of ancient Israel, and other topics treated in these pages. My goal here, as elsewhere in this volume, is to invite reflection on the implications of these debates for Christian biblical theology and faithful reading. Thus I am assuming that you have already read or will consult handbooks on the Documentary Hypothesis as needed in order to orient yourself generally to the issues. Most introductory textbooks about the Hebrew Scriptures can suffice for this purpose.

Before we consider the importance of attentiveness to different literary sources in the Pentateuch, we should consider some of the vulnerabilities in source criticism as a method.

WEAKNESSES OF THE METHOD

Critics of the Documentary Hypothesis have long objected that the proliferation of models within the larger theory itself points to how confused and unclear scholars are about what is going on in the Pentateuch. The so-called Yahwist, J, has been portrayed in biblical scholarship as everything from a brilliant tenth-century-BCE theologian to an exilic redactor to an innovative Hellenistic-era historian. The so-called Elohistic material, E, has been argued to be a continuous source, a series of fragments of tradition, or a layer of supplementations added to the J stratum, and even among those who hold to the Documentary Hypothesis in one modified form or another, you can find folks who don't believe that E exists at all, at least in any kind of discernible and coherent form. Scholars have argued variously that the sources extend only through Numbers (yielding a Tetrateuch), Deuteronomy (and thus a Pentateuch), Joshua (giving us a Hexateuch), and on through Kings (for an Enneateuch). The fact that such significant dimensions of the theory as historical dating, literary extent of the sources, and even existence of certain of the sources are fiercely contested—among those who do support the Documentary Hypothesis, mind you!—makes detractors and outsiders to the discussion wonder whether the "hypothesis" is really anything more than an ongoing series of complicated and perhaps futile arguments.

Further, source criticism has not always been performed with precision and sound logic. As with any method in biblical scholarship, there are skilled practitioners of the method who understand well the logical implications of particular hermeneutical claims and arguments, and there are practitioners who do not wield the method with analytical and exegetical proficiency. This unevenness in performance has sometimes been used to reject the method itself, which is not entirely fair. If someone were to offer an unimpressive literary-critical reading of the book of Jonah, say, demonstrating a tin ear regarding nuances of the Hebrew language or a clumsy way of analyzing dramatic irony or characterization, you would certainly not conclude that literary criticism as a method is completely bankrupt. But sometimes source criticism has been subjected to that kind of blanket dismissal due, at least in part, to the fact that local interpretations are not always well done.

An excellent analysis of methodological errors in the performance of source criticism has been articulated by my colleague, Joel S. Baden.[2] He argues that in the practice of source criticism, the following missteps have adversely affected the overall cogency of the Documentary Hypothesis:

1. Scholars have extrapolated historical and cultural conclusions from the legal material and applied those conclusions to the narratives, when instead source criticism should be conceived and applied as a solely literary method of tracing narrative coherence and discontinuity.
2. Scholars have wrongly assumed that all of the sources would have been telling the same stories, and thus have divided up narratives into impossibly fractured layers in order to render similar accounts in the different sources.
3. Scholars have projected overwrought literary and theological expectations onto a redactor or redactors.

Baden's lengthy discussion provides a welcome refining of source-critical method. It is useful for those thinking about the logic behind different sources in any work of literature, not just the Pentateuch. Baden's work is worthy of careful consideration by any reader of the Pentateuch who thinks about how the text may have reached its final form, and his book is indispensable for scholars who still argue for four discrete written documents underlying the composition of the Pentateuch.

But in my view, no defense of the Documentary Hypothesis has yet fully addressed the serious issue of tautology—circular thinking and arguing—in models of the Documentary Hypothesis. Nor has any defense yet avoided relying on a number of claims made from silence (speculating based on what *doesn't* appear in a source) and a certain convenient "flexibility" about what counts as evidence under varied circumstances. Often in this subfield, you will see claims that rely on narratological and terminological consistency when that is convenient for the argument but eagerly concede the possibility of inconsistency and variation when *that* suits the larger argument better.

2. Joel S. Baden, *J, E, and the Redaction of the Pentateuch* (Tübingen: Mohr Siebeck, 2009).

AROUND AND AROUND WE GO

Here is just one example of a tautological claim, a problem that is multiplied many times over in most works I've seen that support the Documentary Hypothesis: that the E material does not know anything about the ark; therefore if a passage contains a reference to the ark, it cannot be assigned to E.[3] Do you see the circular reasoning there? Over and over again, on many different levels from semantic usage of words to the characterization of special theological interests of J and E to the postulation of larger narratological structures, arguments in favor of the Documentary Hypothesis falter on the basis of tautological and speculative claims. My objections to the theory as a whole do not mean the theory is demonstrably false, just that arguments for it are weaker than is sometimes acknowledged and thus that the theory has not yet been persuasively proved. That's something helpful to keep in mind whenever you read: something may be true, but the evidence just might not allow for decisive proof; or something may be false despite what the evidence seems to suggest. Your own life experience may bear that out. We can't always "prove" what we know to be true, but that does not necessarily make it less true. And we can't always decisively refute something even if it is clearly wrongheaded. I hope you might find that observation helpful in frustrating moments of intellectual conflict or "deconstruction," whether you are learning in a divinity school classroom or simply going through the joys and perils of lifelong learning generally. Trust what you know to be true, even while you open yourself to new ideas and especially when you experience friction between different truths that you have not yet adequately reconciled in your own mind. Wisdom goes far deeper than the absence or presence of contradiction. God's truth is much greater than the models we can develop to describe it.

Let's get back on the merry-go-round for a moment. Circularity of reasoning is nowhere more evident than in the battle over whether there was an Elohist or not. A number of odd or unique pentateuchal traditions have been argued by scholars to represent an Elohist source or editorial layer or collection of fragments and supplementations. Standard among proponents of the Documentary Hypothesis are the assertions that E calls the mountain where the Law was given "Horeb" rather than Sinai, that E is responsible for

3. Baden, disagreeing with attributions of Exod. 33:7–11 to E, mentions two scholars who "accepted the possibility that the instructions regarding the tablets are from E, but noted Wellhausen's suggestion that the 'natural' place for such would have been before E's account of 'the sanctuary which contained the ark' in Exod 33:7–11. This argument falls apart when it is realized that there is no mention at all of the ark in Exod 33:7–11. . . . E, as we have seen, does not in fact contain any reference to the ark whatsoever" (222).

significant portions of the Joseph story in Genesis and the Balaam cycle in Numbers, that E is interested in prophecy, and that E gives us a mysterious God who is revealed through dreams and encounters with angels.

Is the Horeb tradition distinctive? Yes. There is unquestionably an ancient Israelite source that called the mountain of God "Horeb" rather than Sinai, and we see traces of that tradition in our Bible. But are the references to Horeb characteristic of a single, coherent written Elohist source? That's a far different question. The assertion remains unproved that mentions of "Horeb" are consistent in and characteristic of a particular continuous written source. In fact, Baden argues that in at least one instance, "Horeb" is actually used by J, so even the presence of the word "Horeb" as such may not be definitive for source-critical analysis.[4] And the Horeb issue is one of the criteria that lots of source critics take for granted: it's not even one of the more hotly contested issues.

A similar kind of flawed logic is evident in the claim that "only in E is Abraham called a prophet (Gen 20.7)."[5] Only in Genesis 20:7 is Abraham called a prophet. How could this single instance possibly be argued to be characteristic of E or anything else? Even if one were to concede that the passage is to be attributed to E, there is still no way to know whether E preserved this odd designation for Abraham from some earlier or other source. To say that E thinks of Abraham as a prophet and that only in E is Abraham thought of in this way is weak logic. Those examples—about Horeb and Abraham-as-prophet—are only two of numerous examples of poor argumentation that could be cited in the pentateuchal discussions. This is not entirely the fault of the scholars involved in these debates. It's due to the unwieldy, vastly complex structure of claims and suppositions required by the Documentary Hypothesis in order for it to control all of the textual data.

Arguments connecting the various kinds of dreams in the Pentateuch tend to be superficial and tenuous too, if they are articulated in any detail at all. Abram's terrifying experience during a supernatural deep sleep (Gen. 15:12–17) has nothing in common, theologically or literarily, with Jacob's dream at Bethel (28:10–17)—nor do either of those dreams have anything in common with Joseph's narration of dreams about his own power (37:5–11) and his interpretation of the dreams of the cupbearer, baker, and Pharaoh (40:1–41:36). Those three kinds of dream narratives differ dramatically from each other in terms of characterization of the protagonist, the way in which the sequence of the dreams is described, the function of the dream in the larger rhetorical and literary setting of its narrative, the representation of the

4. Ibid., 176–77.

5. Michael D. Coogan, *The Old Testament: A Historical and Literary Introduction to the Hebrew Scriptures* (Oxford: Oxford University Press, 2006), 26; many other scholars make such a claim.

Holy in these dreams, and the thematic connection of the dreams to larger blocks of tradition. That the so-called Elohist is "interested in dreams and dream reports" is a broad and vague claim that becomes virtually meaningless when one pays attention to the diverse ways in which dream, dreamer, narration, and theological concerns play out in those materials.

Also problematic are some of the arguments based on language. Numbers 20:14–21 is assigned to E by Baden because it contains a phrase "otherwise only known from E" (Exod. 18:8) and the phrase "fields and vineyards" is also present in other purported E passages. Though Baden admits that the latter datum can bear only "a supporting role" in an argument for attribution to E,[6] the first point is equally shaky. We cannot assume that anything is proved about authorship of an entire passage simply because a phrase occurs in both Numbers 20:14 and Exodus 18:8. At most, one might be able to argue for literary dependence of one passage on another. But even there, you would need to show not just coincidence of language (however rare) but also that one author's characteristic and unique way of working with prior sources is clearly in evidence here.[7] Saying, as it were, "look, an unusual noun-verb combination in both passages: if one is E, then the other must be, too," is not actual argumentation but just assertion based on circular logic. This is not a critique of Baden per se, whose very fine work brings much-needed clarity to the arguments that proponents of the Documentary Hypothesis offer. It is a critique of the kind of circular logic that is required by the hypothesis itself as hermeneutical model.

"The arguments for an early dating of J and E, and especially for dating J to the first century of the Israelite monarchy, have never been particularly effective over the entire span of the narrative. . . . E has long been problematic, and there is no longer much enthusiasm for retaining it. . . . P has stood up best to scrutiny, because of its more distinctive vocabulary, style, and ideology. . . . It is true that the documentary hypothesis has increasingly been shown to be flawed, and will survive, if at all, only in a greatly modified form, but that does not mean that we should ignore the results of the last two centuries of investigation. Our task is to find better ways of understanding how the Pentateuch came to be without writing off the real advances of our predecessors."

—Joseph Blenkinsopp, *The Pentateuch* (1992), 21–28

6. Baden, *J, E, and the Redaction of the Pentateuch*, 131.

7. See the excellent methodological discussion on determining literary dependence generally in Benjamin D. Sommer, *A Prophet Reads Scripture: Allusion in Isaiah 40–66* (Stanford, CA: Stanford University Press, 1998).

What about the notion of a coherent narrative plotline that encompasses all of the E material? Tautologies abound in arguments for this as well. Sometimes a strong case can be made for distinct stories with their own logic and internal coherence, as with the two flood narratives in Genesis 6–9. There we can clearly see the conflict of actual numbers (pairs of animals, number of days the waters remained on the earth). In many other instances, though, the separation into distinct and whole narratives is less clear. We could consider the story in Numbers 32 of the conquest of the region of Transjordan. Baden argues for two entirely distinct and coherent narratives—E and P—with different motivations and different resolutions, E then being drawn on by D later.[8] But some may not be convinced by the mustering of lexical indicators that include extremely common Hebrew words (the verb *yashav*, the divine name YHWH, and the preposition *liphne'* among them), and Baden rightly concedes that they have only "suggestive" force in the argument. Is it possible to read Numbers 32 as an integrated literary whole rather than the product of two sources spliced together? Certainly, and in fact, such a narrative unfolds with a sophisticated depth of dialogue that is attenuated when the text is divided into two separate sources. The Reubenites and Gadites ask for Gilead for pasturage, and Moses responds with a negative example from their ancestors' story: the ancestors, too, were drawn to the land of Canaan as a fruitful place, flowing with milk and honey, but those sent to scout out the land brought back an unfavorable report, anxious at the prospect of battle with the inhabitants (Num. 13–14). The savvy Reubenites and Gadites respond that they will build folds for their livestock but also take up arms—it

> "Gaps . . . and their expression heighten our sense of disharmony: they bring out the missing link in the chain, the oddity of conduct, the inconsistency or looseness of the official record. . . . Again, the missing psychological link in the dialogic chain may relate not so much to hidden as to second thoughts. Consider how the Reuben and Gad tribes first apply to Moses for exemption from crossing the Jordan and then do an about-face and volunteer 'to go before the people of Israel' throughout the conquest. The leader's intervening (and explicit) tirade must have precipitated another intervening (but implicit) development, in the form of a conviction on the part of the would-be Transjordanians that to achieve their tribal goal they must spearhead rather than shirk the national campaign."
>
> —Meir Sternberg, *The Poetics of Biblical Narrative* (1985), 242, 244

8. Baden, *J, E, and the Redaction of the Pentateuch*, 141–53.

need not be one or the other; after some tense and precise restatements of the conditions of the compromise, Moses and the Transjordanian tribes come to an agreement. Literary critic Meir Sternberg has shown that biblical Hebrew narrative skillfully uses gaps, misdirection, and discursive tensions to convey subtle points about characters and plot developments. In this particular case, we may with ease locate this apparent "problem" on the level of narratorial brilliance rather than source-critical disruption. Whether we hear textual disjuncture or, instead, narratologically purposeful communicative strategies such as cagy redirection and intentional reframing of information—all this depends on the hermeneutic we bring to each text we read.

THE ELOHIST'S LAST DANCE

One final example. The Joseph material is an interesting test case for hermeneutical debates between proponents of source criticism and proponents of literary approaches that presume coherence, preferring to allow an author diverse strategies of communication without leaping to the conclusion that multiple sources or editors were necessarily involved. Martin Noth divides up Genesis 37–50 into highly fractured sources, with passages splintered into verses and even half-verses: J material includes 37:3a, 4, 5a, 6–21, 25–27, 28aβb; all of chapters 38 and 39; 41:34a, 35b, 41–45a, and so on. Special E material, according to Noth, includes all of chapters 40 and 41, Joseph's dreams. To the Priestly writer, Noth ascribes two verses in chapter 37, one verse in chapter 41, much of chapter 46, and a handful of verses in chapters 47, 48, 49, and 50.[9] Now, some of these source-critical observations are certainly correct. In chapter 46, we have a long Priestly genealogy that starts, "Now these are the names of the Israelites, Jacob and his offspring, who came to Egypt . . . ," and then lists Reuben and his children, Simeon and his children, and on through the twelve tribes. That is certainly a Priestly interpolation—no doubt about it. But there are other issues that are not so easily resolved by standard source criticism. Is there any possible way to separate out all of the dream material in the Joseph story as Elohist, as if it were a distinct and coherent other source? Or another example: when Joseph is being sold by his brothers into slavery, there are divergent traditions about the traders who took care of the transaction: were they Ishmaelites or Midianites? We have two different traditions here, but they cannot be equated with source-critical distinctions in any obvious way—not without lots of special pleading.[10]

9. From Martin Noth's *A History of Pentateuch Traditions*, trans. Bernhard W. Anderson (Atlanta: Scholars Press, 1981), 18 and 35–36.

10. So also Collins, *Introduction to the Hebrew Bible*, 101.

The most important point one might make about Genesis 37–50 is not, in fact, about the minor discrepancies that crop up but about the style and theological tenor of the whole, which are quite unlike anything that has gone before in Genesis. Joseph Blenkinsopp worries that we should not overstate the distinctiveness of the Joseph material, because it is connected to the earlier parts of Genesis by means of broad themes, including the family history of Abraham, sibling rivalry, and "the birth of sons."[11] But another reader might object that these sorts of connections are so broadly painted across such radically different literary styles as to be only weakly significant. And Blenkinsopp does concede that "the highly individual character of the Joseph story and the difficulty of reducing it to a combination of J and E have been widely acknowledged."[12] Indeed, scholars have long suggested that the Joseph material may have had its own independent transmission history apart from the rest of Genesis. Claus Westermann says that standard source criticism does not help here:

> The Yahwist is not the author of the Joseph story. . . . The working method and style are so basically different from that of J in chs. 12–36 that one must look for another author. The most important difference is that J put together his work out of narratives, genealogies, and itineraries that came down to him, and was the actual author only of certain introductory and concluding pieces, scenes, or links; but the author of the Joseph story composed a narrative in writing from the very beginning; he undoubtedly used several well known narrative motifs, but not traditional oral narratives.[13]

Consider the observation of Fretheim that Joseph "associates with no centers of worship and builds no altars."[14] This is very different indeed from the foundational stories of Abraham and Jacob building altars and encountering God at cult sites. Jon D. Levenson remarks that the theology of the Joseph story is markedly different from that of the Yahwist or the Elohist: "Whereas the patriarchal narrative is replete with appearances of God or His messengers, and oracles from them, Joseph never sees or hears God or His messengers. . . . Rather, God works here in a hidden way, secretly guiding the course of human events."[15] Right. While we do have a few obvious Priestly and other additions in Genesis 37–50, a strong case can be made that we should move away from thinking about J , E, or a combined JE document here.

11. Joseph Blenkinsopp, *The Pentateuch* (New York: Doubleday, 1992), 107.

12. Ibid., 124.

13. Claus Westermann, *Genesis 37–50*, trans. John J. Scullion (Minneapolis: Augsburg Pub. House, 1986), 28.

14. Terence E. Fretheim, *The Pentateuch* (Nashville: Abingdon Press, 1996), 91.

15. Jon D. Levenson, in annotations to Genesis for *The Jewish Study Bible*, ed. Adele Berlin and Marc Zvi Brettler (Oxford: Oxford University Press, 2004).

> "I believe that the traditional Documentary Hypothesis has come to an end. Of course, there are still attempts to save the Yahwist, and even the Elohist, whose existence had been questioned much earlier. But I do not see any new arguments that could turn back the wheel. . . . Old Testament scholarship at present is 'in crisis.'"
>
> —Rolf Rendtorff, "The Paradigm Is Changing—Hopes and Fears" (1999), 60

The few examples of tautology I have mustered above could be multiplied many times over, depending on which local instance of argumentation for the Documentary Hypothesis one examines.

THINKING ANEW ABOUT MULTIPLE SOURCES

Do you want to get off the merry-go-round? David M. Carr sees a new consensus emerging in pentateuchal criticism, one that shakes the foundations of the older Documentary Hypothesis. The hallmarks of this new consensus are two: first, a conviction that the ancestral traditions and the Moses traditions—Genesis and Exodus, essentially—were unconnected to each other until late in ancient Israel's history (the exilic period or later); and second, a rejection of the notion that there was a preexilic Yahwist responsible for crafting a full narrative of Israel's origins. In a concluding reflection for a 2006 collection of essays by leading pentateuchal scholars, Carr writes,

> Whether one agrees with Schmid, Gertz, and Römer that P was the first to join ancestors and Moses in a literary whole or agrees with me and others that a late pre-Priestly author/editor created the first proto-Pentateuch, there is agreement that . . . the ancestral and the exodus traditions were separate most of the preexilic period, if not also through much of the exilic period as well. . . . No one in the present volume works with the idea of an early preexilic "Yahwistic" proto-Pentateuch nor with an E source.[16]

The ongoing scholarly arguments about J and E underline the fascinating ways in which the prose, poetic, and legal traditions of the Hebrew

16. David M. Carr, "What Is Required to Identify Pre-Priestly Narrative Connections between Genesis and Exodus? Some General Reflections and Specific Cases," in *A Farewell to the Yahwist? The Composition of the Pentateuch in Recent European Interpretation*, ed. Thomas B. Dozeman and Konrad Schmid (Leiden: E. J. Brill, 2006), 179–80.

Scriptures resist easy classification. Does glimpsing all this lively and detailed debate make you just want to throw up your hands and say, "Who cares?" Or, as with that student prayer leader in chapel worship, does it make you feel that your belief in the integrity of Scripture is being undermined? Before you give up or push back, let me invite you to consider that it does matter, deeply, whether and how we hear multiple voices within Scripture, even if we disagree about how to define those voices. It is beyond dispute that many ancient traditions are preserved in the Pentateuch. Some may be organized in blocks of tradition or specific themes that then grew in a whole variety of ways over time; scholars such as Rolf Rendtorff, Erhard Blum, and Antony F. Campbell and Mark O'Brien have put forward proposals in this vein. Some of Israel's ancient traditions may be located within clearly distinct streams of tradition (P and D); others may reflect vastly divergent theological, cultural, and literary interests from many different contexts within the life of ancient Israel. This in no way compromises the theological authority of the Hebrew Scriptures. Perhaps the worst it can do is to throw a monkey wrench into a reader's uncritical acceptance of the teaching of her denomination, if that denomination is wedded to the ancient idea—never claimed anywhere in Scripture itself—that Moses wrote the Pentateuch. In a beautiful and powerful way, multiple witnesses within the Bible serve to confirm, not disconfirm, the historical rootedness of these different memories of Israel's encounters with God.

Debates about the composition of the Pentateuch have raised important questions about ways in which the sources may or may not presuppose an integrated narrative about Israel's origins, cultural identity, and experiences of the Holy. If the narratives are not unified and do not necessarily presuppose each other (except as may be seen in late editorial "bridges" and additions), and if the sources are themselves not as unified and coherent as some proponents of the classical Documentary Hypothesis claim, what does this mean for our understanding of the story of Israel's origins? And what does it mean for our faith in the God to whom the Scriptures point?

Each reader will need to meet those issues on her own terms, as she journeys through and with Scripture. But as preparation for the journey, I would like to offer three reflections on positive aspects of the question.

HONORING DIVERSE WITNESSES

First, we may embrace the opportunity to grapple with the fact that Scripture honors diverse witnesses to the action of God in the life of ancient Israel. I use "grapple" here in its positive, energizing sense. The spiritual effects of "wrestling" hermeneutically may be metaphorically similar to the way in which physical exercise beneficially raises one's heart rate, respiration rate, and alertness. For the reader who cherishes Scripture as sacred, all of these traditions are true in particular ways unique to their own witness and their own context. Every single source—whether a broad stream of tradition or a quirky, idiosyncratic isolated reference—is dedicated to illuminating the formation of Israel's communal identity through its engagement with the God who has called Israel in love.

The Priestly material emphasizes the transcendent creative power of God as that may be encountered through faithful ritual observance, joyful submission in the face of God's ineffable holiness, remembrance of the enduring value of community through the preservation of genealogical lines of Israelite families, and so on. The Deuteronomistic material celebrates the reciprocal nature of covenant and the unshakable faithfulness and reliability of God, the fulfillment of prophecies as demonstration of the efficacy of God's mighty Word, God's continued commitment to future generations of Israel through the raising up of prophetic leaders for God's people, and so on. The non-Priestly material is interested in—well, too many things to sum up easily. In the so-called J and E material, we can see dialogical relationship unfolding between chosen individuals and God as paradigmatic for the life of faith; the salutary fear of God pointing toward the radical wildness and unpredictability of the One with whom Israel is in covenant; awareness of the potent dangers that loom in those liminal moments in which the believer decides whether faithfulness or self-interest is more compelling; and much more. The conversation among Priestly traditions, Deuteronomistic traditions, and other non-Priestly materials (so-called J, so-called E, and other) is far richer than any one kind of source could have fostered on its own.

GRATITUDE FOR FRUITFUL TENSIONS

A second reflection: we may inhabit a spiritual posture of deep gratitude for the moments of fruitful tension and contestation among different Scriptural witnesses. Why gratitude? Because as Christian theology has recognized since the composition of the New Testament, no one diction or set of commands or story about God can speak the full and entire truth of God. Believers need to understand that well, if they are not to fall into the trap of misunderstanding who God is, fetishizing a partial truth or making an idol out of one particular segment of the larger picture. The frictions and creative tensions among multiple witnesses to God's truth require that the attentive reader move beyond idolatrous reification of any one particular view of God or mode of engagement with God. God's truth is beyond human comprehension and beyond the limits of human language.

What would have been lost if the unique Priestly witness had not been preserved? We would have missed testimony to the expansive cosmic scope of God's creative action and ways in which that divine creativity may be honored and responded to in liturgy and ritual observance. We would not have heard ancient reflections on a world that was elegantly structured in terms of the liturgical calendar and in terms of the kinds of creatures with which God's beloved people orders its ritual life. God's battle over the forces of chaos and death would not have been reframed for us as it is in Genesis 1, where many scholars hear a subtle allusion to God having dominion over the Deep and the luminaries in the heavens. Whether you hear that primordial "battle" as mythopoetic or metaphorical or spiritual, we may surely agree that not to have the Priestly creation account would have drastically impoverished the imaginations of believers. Or consider the power of God's command to the faithful to "be holy, for I the LORD your God am holy" (Lev. 19:2). What do those words mean to you? Even though Christians are no longer bound by the halakic dimensions of the law, many Christians have found those words from Leviticus to be important for their personal lives of devotion and for the discipline of moral theology. Through the centuries, that passage has been profoundly formative in Christian traditions of monasticism and asceticism. Surely many believers could not live as joyfully as they do without that invitation to enter into the holiness of the God who sanctifies all of our living. Listen to Israel Knohl about the power of the Priestly witness:

> Only in the Priestly Torah do we find a systematic avoidance of the attribution of any physical dimensions to God and of almost any action of God, save the act of commanding. The Priestly thinkers attained an astounding level of abstraction and sublimity. That such a conception develops at the early stages of Israelite monotheism, long before the rise of Greek philosophy, is indeed startling. The course of Israelite religion is not—as so many writers from the nineteenth century claimed—an incremental evolution from the primitive, coarse, and opaque to the pure and the refined. Rather, it can be argued that the purest and most refined elements appeared right at an early stage.[17]

The Deuteronomic material is the very heart of the law: robust and passionate covenant, articulated with a deep and enduring intentionality and demanded of all those who would know God. Without D, we would lose

17. Israel Knohl, *The Divine Symphony: The Bible's Many Voices* (Philadelphia: Jewish Publication Society, 2003), 9.

Israel's most defined structuring of sacred history according to the purposes of God, to whom the prophets pointed and whom kings either obeyed or defied. The Deuteronomistic trajectory or stream of tradition is powerfully present throughout the Hebrew Scriptures, because Deuteronomistic editors had a hand in shaping many biblical books.

What would have been the cost if the other non-Priestly material—those traditions that supporters of the Documentary Hypothesis have termed J and E—had been excluded from Scripture in the ancient processes of composition? Without those texts that some scholars attribute to E, we would lose precious and unusual dimensions of Israel's testimony to the mystery of God. With the so-called Yahwistic material we see a God who creates out of dust, who talks with Adam and Eve, who argues with Abraham; a God who is known in the messiness and process and tensions of intimate relationship. Hear how Gerhard von Rad rhapsodizes about the contributions of the J source:

> As regards the creative genius of the *Yahwist's narrative* there is only admiration. Someone has justly called the artistic mastery in this narrative one of the greatest accomplishments of all times in the history of thought. Wonderful clarity and utter simplicity characterize the representation of the individual scenes. The meagerness of his resources is truly amazing, and yet this narrator's view encompasses the whole of human life with all its heights and depths. With unrivalled objectivity he has made man the subject of his presentation—both the riddles and conflicts of his visible acts and ways of behaving as well as the mistakes and muddles in the secret of his heart. He among the biblical writers is the great psychologist. . . . In the primeval history he subjects the great problems of humanity to the light of revelation: creation and nature, sin and suffering, man and wife, fraternal quarrels, international confusion, etc. . . . The Yahwistic narrative is full of the boldest anthropomorphisms. Yahweh walks in the garden in the cool of the evening; he himself closes the ark; he descends to inspect the Tower of Babel, etc. This is anything but the bluntness and naïveté of an archaic narrator. It is, rather, the candor and lack of hesitation which is only the mark of a lofty and mature way of thinking.[18]

By bringing these distinct voices together, our sacred texts compel us to engage multiple ways of understanding divine agency and the person of God. The Holy is not definable, nor can it be commodified by any one complex of metaphors, one set of apodictic commands, or one kind of storytelling. The more often we are reminded of this, the better! It is when we listen carefully, staying present to generative tensions among different scriptural voices, that

18. Gerhard von Rad, *Genesis*, Old Testament Library (Philadelphia: Westminster Press, 1972), 25–26, with original emphasis.

we can best understand the witness of the whole. To blur all of these testimonies together into a flat, monolithic single speech would be costly indeed.

THE ETHICS OF ATTENDING TO DIFFERENT VOICES

A third reflection for the hermeneutical journey: attending with care to the different ancient witnesses we hear in Scripture is a matter of central importance for Christian ethics. Early and late, biblical texts exhort the faithful to social justice: passionate advocacy on behalf of the poor, pastoral care with the marginalized and the voiceless. Deuteronomic language for lifting up the disempowered focuses on the "sojourner," the "widow," and the "orphan." In the prophetic corpus, the focus is often on ending oppression of or callousness toward "the poor." Whatever language is used, we know that believers are expected to attend to the needs of all in the community, and especially those who have no voice in cultural centers of power (the royal court, the public square, the academy). It is a fundamental truth that no one voice can speak accurately or fully for all in the human community. When one voice is allowed to hold forth in monologue, others are necessarily silenced. It is ethically incumbent upon the people of God, therefore, to listen for multiple testimonies within Scripture as a means of honoring as many voices, lived experiences, and witnesses to the truth of God as we possibly can.

> "The truth about human nature, the world, and God *cannot* be uttered by a single voice but only by a community of unmerged voices."
> —Carol A. Newsom, "Bakhtin, the Bible, and Dialogic Truth" (1996), 301, with original emphasis

Thus for hermeneutical, theological, and ethical reasons, we should attend carefully to the dialogical expression of truth in Scripture. It is my conviction that the church will benefit richly if we do so. This can be true whether you still hold to the Documentary Hypothesis or (like me) you have doubts concerning fundamental aspects of the theory and prefer to think of the non-Priestly and non-Deuteronomic material in terms of streams of tradition or blocks of thematically organized material. However you conceive of the material, we have voices in dialogue. Two thinkers who can help us appreciate dialogical witness are biblical theologian Walter Brueggemann and philosopher Mikhail Bakhtin.

WALTER BRUEGGEMANN: TESTIMONY AND COUNTERTESTIMONY

The books of biblical scholar Walter Brueggemann may have done more to keep pastors and churchgoers engaged with biblical scholarship than has anything else written in this generation. Born in Nebraska, Brueggemann enjoyed a broad-based educational training, earning an AB in sociology from Elmhurst College, a BD in Old Testament from Eden Theological Seminary, a ThD in Old Testament from Union Theological Seminary, and a PhD in education from St. Louis University. He was ordained in the Evangelical Reformed Church, an antecedent of the United Church of Christ, and in latter years has worshiped in Episcopal churches. His prolific writings on the Old Testament always start from a place of textual engagement rather than, say, privileging the history of Israelite religion or working from abstract systematic propositions. Brueggemann characteristically moves from exegetical soundings to larger theological claims.

It is a hallmark of his work that he honors tensions and moments of friction that he discerns in the biblical text, rather than working to resolve them in an artificial synthesis. Brueggemann has turned his attention to the rhetoric of the Hebrew Scriptures, inveighing sharply against positivist historical interpretation en route. He may not have navigated entirely safely the shoals of historicist thinking himself, something he freely concedes: "I am sure that I have not done well in articulating the delicate relationship between historical criticism and theological exposition. Part of the problem is that I am so deeply situated in historical criticism that it is likely that I appeal much more to such categories than I am aware."[19] But no reader of Brueggemann's oeuvre can fail to be alert to the risks of allowing historicist assumptions about biblical interpretation to go unexamined.

Tentative and conflicted claims within Scripture compel Brueggemann's exegetical attention. He has written on the formation of alternative community via prophetic diction (*The Prophetic Imagination*, 1978; 2nd ed., 2001); the divergent presentations of David discernible in Scripture (*David's Truth in Israel's Imagination and Memory*, 1985); ways in which marginality and pain may be powerful catalysts for the evangelical imagination (*Interpretation and Obedience: From Faithful Reading to Faithful Living*, 1991); local, provisional interpretation of Scripture texts as the key to persuasive preaching of the Gospel in a postmodern world (*Texts under Negotiation: The Bible and Postmodern Imagination*, 1993); and the importance of relinquishing our need for

19. Walter Brueggemann, "Theology of the Old Testament: A Prompt Retrospect," in *God in the Fray: A Tribute to Walter Brueggemann*, ed. Tod Linafelt and Timothy K. Beal (Minneapolis: Fortress Press, 1998), 315.

security and certitude in order to embrace the unsettling, transformative ways of God (see *Mandate to Difference: An Invitation to the Contemporary Church*, 2007—and many other Brueggemann works).

One of the most important contributions Brueggemann has made to biblical theology is his articulation of a model for understanding the diversity of witnesses we encounter in the Hebrew Scriptures. Brueggemann sees Scripture as a dynamic arena—which he likens to a courtroom—in which various testimonies and countertestimonies about God are heard and adjudicated. He lays out this extended testimony metaphor in detail in his massive *Theology of the Old Testament: Testimony, Dispute, Advocacy* (1997). God is made real through the rhetorical practices of Israel in its Scriptures—through Israel's speech. That is to say, God is "uttered" in a variety of ways, with some perspectives contesting others and some accounts conflicting with other accounts. These utterances together make up the multivocal dialogue that is the witness of the Hebrew Scriptures. According to Brueggemann, the dialogue is open-ended and volatile within the pages of Scripture; no one textual voice "wins" or can command the field for long.

> "The God of Israel is characteristically 'in the fray' and at risk in the ongoing life of Israel. . . . Israel's text, and therefore Israel and Israel's God, are always in the middle of an exchange, unable to come to ultimate resolution. There may be momentary or provisional resolution, but because both parties are intensely engaged and are so relentlessly verbal, we are always sure that there will be another speech, another challenge, another invitation, another petition, another argument, which will reopen the matter and expend the provisional settlement. Thus Israel's religious rhetoric does not intend to reach resolution or to achieve closure."
>
> —Walter Brueggemann, *Theology of the Old Testament* (1997), 83

Brueggemann identifies what he calls Israel's "core testimony" in a variety of rhetorics within the Hebrew Scriptures. This normative testimony includes thanksgiving for God's righteousness and covenant faithfulness; praise of God for the divine power to create, redeem, and transform; assertion of God's incomparability, sovereignty, constancy, and invincibility; affirmation of God's commitment to act on behalf of the powerless and against the wicked; and statements of confidence in God's compassion and love. For example, we may consider as "core testimony" Hannah's song (1 Sam. 2:1–10), which affirms that God is incomparably mighty and wise, that God reverses the fortunes of the arrogant rich and the humble poor, and that God will guard the faithful, including Israel's anointed king. In the Psalms, core testimony is supplied by what Brueggemann calls the "psalms of orientation," psalms that extol and praise God or that express an unshakable trust in God's providence.[20] Examples include Psalm 19, which affirms that creation testifies to God's glory and lauds God's law, God's torah (instruction), as perfect; Psalm 62, in which the psalmist exhorts the congregation to trust in God as fortress and refuge; and the psalms at the end of the Psalter (146–150), which brim with robust praise of God for God's justice, compassion, and matchless power.

Then Brueggemann identifies what he calls Israel's "countertestimony," claims of scriptural witnesses that seem to object to and cross-examine the normative statements described above. Here we encounter Israel's anguished questions about the hiddenness and injustice of God; protests concerning the unmerited severity of divine punishment; anxiety about the ambiguous, contradictory, and potentially deceptive character of God; complaints that God has not been faithful to the covenant with Israel; resistance to God's alarming capacity for violence; and so on. Literature of dissent such as the books of Job and Ecclesiastes would fall in this category of "countertestimony." Also deemed resistant to Israel's normative claims are what Brueggemann calls the "psalms of disorientation," psalms that express the speaker's destabilization or lack of confidence in an all-powerful and consistently merciful God. Examples include Psalm 44, with its persistent claim that God has abandoned God's people without cause; Psalm 74, in which the community cries to God out of its experience of trauma at the hands of an apparently victorious enemy; and Psalm 88, which begins and ends in spiritual darkness.

> "We are now able to recognize, against any hypothesis of a unilateral development of Israel's religion or Israel's 'God-talk,' that the texts themselves witness to a plurality of testimonies concerning God and Israel's life with God. . . . It is, moreover, clear that the several testimonies to Yahweh, in any particular moment of Israel's life, were often in profound dispute with one another, disagreeing from the ground up about the 'truth' of Yahweh. . . . It is the process of dispute and compromise itself that constitutes Israel's mode of theological testimony."
>
> —Brueggemann, *Theology of the Old Testament*, 710

20. See Brueggemann, "Psalms and the Life of Faith: A Suggested Typology of Function," in *The Psalms and the Life of Faith*, ed. Patrick D. Miller (Minneapolis: Fortress Press, 1995), 3–32.

In addition to core testimony and countertestimony, two other kinds of forensic material are described in Brueggemann's hermeneutical framework: Israel's "unsolicited" testimony and Israel's "embodied" testimony. Unsolicited testimony constitutes extra information about YHWH being both free and passionate in relationship with Israel, individuals, the nations, and creation. Brueggemann cites Hosea 11 and Isaiah 44 on God's having chosen Israel-the-child or Israel-the-servant in love, texts in the Psalms and Ezekiel about the beauty of the temple, passages such as Genesis 1 and Psalm 8 about the human dominion over creation, and texts such as Isaiah 2:1–5 // Micah 4:1–4 about the nations partnering with YHWH. Israel's embodied testimony includes such things as the personal encounters of Abraham, Moses, and Elijah with God, the dynamic and open-ended mediation provided by the Torah, the divine governance provided through Israelite and Judean kingship, and the concrete theopolitical engagements of the prophets in their societies.

Brueggemann insists that Israel's testimony, taken as a whole, points to a God who is far more powerful—even just in the biblical text—than can be described or contained by the rubrics of historical criticism, Enlightenment epistemological categories, or systematic theology. According to Brueggemann, the work of interpretation necessarily requires daring imagination. Readers and hearers are invited by the Hebrew Scriptures into complex truths about God and community and the self that are bold and unconstrained by the limitations of particular theological, social, and political logics. Every testimony within Scripture is met by other kinds of biblical testimony and counterclaims. The interactions between and among witnesses within the Hebrew Scriptures, in Brueggemann's hermeneutical model, are robustly dynamic and dialogical across biblical books and across parts of the biblical canon. In his courtroom metaphor, provisional "verdicts" may be reached, but cases are always open to fresh appeals and new contestations. As Fretheim puts it, "Brueggemann's understanding of Israel's God does not fit neatly into systematic categories, not least because he allows himself to be pushed and pulled around by specific texts, and the texts will not sit still any more than he will."[21] The mystery of God's person and action in the life of Israel will never be fully solved or definitively explained to the satisfaction of all (biblical) parties. And so the lively dialogue of claims and counterclaims continues. And the task of interpretation continues as well, reenergized for a church committed to proclamation in the postmodern world.

Throughout his work on biblical rhetoric and contested languages about God, Brueggemann demands that we attend to the agonistic density of the

21. Terence E. Fretheim, "Some Reflections on Brueggemann's God," in Linafelt and Beal, *God in the Fray*, 25.

biblical text. It is not just that *we* struggle as we negotiate the intersections and missed opportunities of biblically grounded life. Our sacred texts struggle, too. His courtroom metaphor requires that any who would adjudicate the biblical evidence listen closely to the Bible's multiple theological dictions, which can differ wildly and sharply from one another as they work to "utter" a transcendent and unsettled God intimately engaged with the life of Israel and the world. Brueggemann's writing is eloquent and catalytic. He gives us a view of sacred Scripture that allows for—even thrives on—the ambiguity, paradox, and uncertainness of life in community.

There remain yet other dimensions of polyphonic meaning to be discerned in the utterances of ancient Israel. Mikhail M. Bakhtin can help us explore certain kinds of complexity in the voicing of biblical texts that are not fully accounted for by Brueggemann's metaphor of individual witnesses offering their testimony.

MIKHAIL BAKHTIN: DIALOGICAL READING

Starting in the 1990s, literary-critical interpretation of the Hebrew Scriptures has been increasingly influenced by Bakhtin's work on narrative and genre.[22] Bakhtin was interested in the inherent "heteroglossia" that we can discern in the functioning of language. What is heteroglossia? One definition I've seen would cause eye-rolling for sure among those who don't like jargon, but here it is: multilanguagedness. It may not technically be a word, but it's a useful neologism! In a nutshell, "heteroglossia" means the several linguistic codes or dictions that can be at play in any apparently unified language. Here is the definition supplied by prominent Bakhtin scholar Michael Holquist:

> HETEROGLOSSIA: The base condition governing the operation of meaning in any utterance. It is that which [ensures] the primacy of context over text. At any given time, in any given place, there will be a set of conditions—social, historical, meteorological, physiological—that will [ensure] that a word uttered in that place and at that time will have a meaning different than it would under any other conditions; all utterances are heteroglot in that they are functions of a matrix of forces practically impossible to recoup, and therefore impossible to resolve.[23]

There are several important ways in which language can be what Bakhtin called "double-voiced." (Here some of us might prefer to use the word

22. A helpful guide here is Barbara Green's *Mikhail Bakhtin and Biblical Scholarship: An Introduction* (Atlanta: Society of Biblical Literature, 2000).

23. Michael Holquist, ed., *The Dialogic Imagination: Four Essays*, by Mikhail M. Bakhtin, trans. Caryl Emerson and Michael Holquist (Austin: University of Texas Press, 1981), 428.

"multivocal," because voicing with its latent or overt intertextual associations and its underlying or implicit countervoices should not be limited conceptually to only two kinds of voices.) The act of expressing ideas and even single words in language always implies dialogical relationship, according to Bakhtin, because no utterance can be offered in a cultural or linguistic vacuum. Every metaphor or other trope in a piece of literature, every character's voice, even an ostensibly simple noun or verb—any of these has meaning only within a web of cultural and linguistic associations, including options or alternatives for meaning that have not been consciously chosen by the author.

> "Language—like the living concrete environment in which the consciousness of the verbal artist lives—is never unitary. It is unitary only as an abstract grammatical system of normative forms, taken in isolation from the concrete, ideological conceptualizations that fill it, and in isolation from the uninterrupted process of historical becoming that is a characteristic of all living language."
>
> —Mikhail M. Bakhtin, "Discourse in the Novel" (1981), 288

According to Bakhtinian dialogism, the signifying of meaning is always a fluid and multidimensional process. Meaning exceeds the control of the author and the control of the interpreter. "Alien" meanings—potential alternative meanings—are present in every text, crowding around the ostensible utterance and pressing it to define itself over against what it is not. Meaning in language can never be fully commodified in service of an author's particular program, because it always has had a prior existence with and among the utterances of others. As Bakhtin puts it, "As a living, socio-ideological concrete thing, as heteroglot opinion, language, for the individual consciousness, lies on the borderline between oneself and the other. The word in language is half someone else's."[24]

> "The word is born in a dialogue as a living rejoinder within it; the word is shaped in dialogic interaction with an alien word that is already in the object. A word forms a concept of its own object in a dialogic way."
>
> —Bakhtin, "Discourse in the Novel," 279

Bakhtin's work can profitably be used to amplify Brueggemann's courtroom metaphor precisely because Bakhtin attends to levels of signification

24. Mikhail M. Bakhtin, "Discourse in the Novel," in ibid., 293.

that are transacted at a deeper level than that of the (metaphorical) designated speaker of testimony. Plurality of voicing may be discerned and interpreted within a single source because that source is relying on one or more genres and other dimensions of cultural-linguistic coding. Genres host literary and cultural valences related to the structuring of the forms themselves and cultural norms, whether those norms are ancient or contemporary and whether the norms are yielded to or contested or subverted in a particular utterance. Genres are deployed in fascinating ways in the biblical corpus; the Hebrew Scriptures contain literatures from many different social groups and settings through several centuries. Numerous examples could be cited of the ways in which genres are alluded to and subverted in biblical literature. The stories of Daniel's sojourns in the fiery furnace and the lions' den may be modeled on the genre of martyrdom story, but in the book of Daniel, the hero is not actually martyred: he lives! The book redirects genre expectations in the implied audience by having the protagonist be exemplary not in his faithful and courageous death but in his continuing to witness wisely and prophetically in life in diaspora. The book of Amos is brilliant at utilizing genres in innovative ways—for example, turning the ancient form of the oracle against a foreign nation also against Judah and Israel themselves (Amos 1–2) and using doxologies that laud God in ways that make increasingly clear God's terrifying power to destroy (Amos 4:13; 5:8–9; and 9:5–6). Qohelet juxtaposes wisdom sayings in ways that seem designed not to promote the monologic statement of sapiential truth but to enhance the audience's experience of contradictions in his argument.

Several biblical scholars have used Bakhtin's insights about genre and double voicing in their interpretation of biblical texts. An important appropriation of Bakhtin can be seen in the work of Carol A. Newsom on dialogism in Job. In *The Book of Job: Contest of Moral Imaginations* (2003), Newsom explores the interplay among the monologic moral diction of the prose framework of Job, the privileging of dissent as part of wisdom in the poetic dialogues between Job and his friends, and the power of Job's first-person testimony about his lived experience. Or consider the work of Carleen Mandolfo on Lamentations and the Psalms. In *God in the Dock: Dialogic Tension in the Psalms of Lament* (2003), Mandolfo counterposes the didactic voice of Deuteronomistic theological orthodoxy in the Psalms to the voice of the lamenting supplicant, arguing that the theological texture of relevant psalms is all the richer for the interplay of these unmerged voices. In *Daughter Zion Talks Back to the Prophets: A Dialogic Theology of the Book of Lamentations* (2007), Mandolfo argues that where the prophetic corpus sexually objectifies and silences Daughter Zion (Jerusalem), in Lamentations Zion resists her characterization in those terms and reconfigures her own identity as a bereaved mother who has been punished disproportionately by God.

Bakhtin's theorizing of genre and other aspects of semantic meaning has been enormously generative in biblical studies, and more fruit will certainly be borne as biblical scholars continue to reflect on his work. Along with Bakhtinian efforts to interpret the multivocal nature of biblical signifying, we may include studies of irony, parody, and humor in biblical texts.[25] All those dimensions of signifying rely on complex rhetorical interactions between what is said and what is left unspoken or assumed by the implied audience. An utterance can never be heard or read without, as it were, already having been interpreted according to norms of language at the levels of grammar, syntax, genre, and larger cultural forces; and every utterance is already refracted through the hopes and prejudices and commitments and misunderstandings of the hearer or reader. Thus every word already harbors infinite "foreignness" within its own performance as an act of communication in a real community and across time and culture. And we should recognize that the "dialogue" going on within and among utterances is not necessarily a creative or constructive dialogue. Sometimes texts and utterances are violently divided within themselves or against another. As we consider the usefulness of Bakhtin's notion of dialogism for reading the story of Jael and Sisera, we would do well to be mindful of this comment by Julia Kristeva: "Dialogue the French way isn't intended to establish a consensus, but to surprise, to reveal, to innovate. . . . And, anyway, psychoanalysis tells us that there is no dialogue, just desires clashing, forces colliding."[26]

Intertextuality is relevant here as well. An infinitely rich and elusive web of connections, influences, and resistances affects the generation of each new text, whether this is recognized by the text's author or not. The universe of intertextual relations also conditions the ways in which every text, old or new, is heard and interpreted. The Psalm 22 that was read by Jesus in first-century Palestine is not the same as the Psalm 22 read by Rashi in eleventh-century France, since the latter was reading after a much fuller tradition of rabbinic interpretation had developed and after Jewish readers became keenly aware of the christological readings of Psalm 22 offered in the New Testament and early Christian apologetics.

The story of Jael and Sisera does not display literary fault lines traditionally associated with the Documentary Hypothesis. Whatever Judges 4 and 5 are—probably very ancient poetic material in Judges 5 and a later narrative recasting in Judges 4—they are not Yahwistic, Elohistic, or Priestly. They are not characteristically Deuteronomistic in any thoroughgoing way either, although we can see that in the final form of Judges, chapters 4–5 are introduced and framed within the larger Deuteronomistic History, and the prose

25. See my *Irony and Meaning in the Hebrew Bible* and the literature cited there on biblical irony, sarcasm, and humor.

26. Kristeva, *Revolt, She Said*, 51.

"The living utterance, having taken meaning and shape at a particular historical moment in a socially specific environment, cannot fail to brush up against thousands of living dialogic threads, woven by socio-ideological consciousness around the given object of an utterance; it cannot fail to become an active participant in social dialogue. After all, the utterance arises out of this dialogue as a continuation of it and as a rejoinder to it—it does not approach the object from the sidelines.

"The way in which the word conceptualizes its object is a complex act—all objects, open to dispute and overlain as they are with qualifications, are from one side highlighted while from the other side dimmed by heteroglot social opinion, by an alien word about them. And into this complex play of light and shadow the word enters—it becomes saturated with this play, and must determine within it the boundaries of its own semantic and stylistic contours."

—Bakhtin, "Discourse in the Novel," 276–77

account certainly has details that accord with the Deuteronomistic holy-war ethos. Nevertheless, these two versions of the same event clearly represent two distinct sources or articulations of tradition. So consideration of their diverse witnesses can be helpful, by analogy, for our purposes here.

Judges 4 spins out the narrative in dramatic storytelling mode, as it unfolds. Israel is in dire straits, oppressed by Jabin; the prophet Deborah summons Barak and decisively lays out the battle strategy, which will be carried out by the tribes of Naphtali and Zebulun; the LORD throws the Canaanites into a panic, and they are routed by Barak's forces; Sisera flees to Jael and collapses with exhaustion, whereupon Jael executes the sleeping warrior. Judges 5 offers a different diction in several key respects. The entire event is narrated as part of a epic victory song sung in praise of God, so the outcome is already known; the mustering of six willing Israelite tribes and the apparent hesitation of four others are recounted in detail (only ten tribes here, and some are named with ancient names—Judges 5 is likely older than the time at which the tradition of the twelve tribes of Israel became standard); cosmic dimensions of the battle are hymned; an alert, standing Sisera is killed by Jael; and a sharply ironic note is introduced with the vignette of Sisera's mother watching in vain for the return of her son and musing on the plundering and raping that he must be doing. Analyzing all of the differences between the prose and poetic accounts would require a monograph. Here I shall have to content myself with sketching some brief observations that are, I hope, suggestive of Brueggemannesque and Bakhtinian readings.

First, we may hear these chapters as testimony and countertestimony. The holy-war testimony of Judges 4 is strong and confident, vivid with theological certitude and painted in rhetorically bold strokes. Barak's anxiety might look like weakness on the part of Israel: as J. Clinton McCann says, the chief commander of Israel's forces is "a guy named 'Lightning,' who seems none too quick, brave, or brilliant."[27] But his character may be read as a foil that points up the strength and decisiveness of all of the other characters allied with Israel (Deborah, Jael, and God). Israel acts as one, unified under the unwavering leadership of the glorious Deborah. Barak calls, and ten thousand troops are immediately with him; they rout the Canaanites in the space of a few verses and ultimately destroy Jabin. Monologic surety indeed: God's holy people are victorious in combat, with the LORD, the Divine Warrior, at their side!

Judges 5, though, is a different telling. It is not fully "counter" in its theology, for the God of Israel is still sovereign here. But this is unsolicited testimony from an Israel that begins to provide too much information in the elaborate poetry, and it does counter the Judges 4 portrayal of Israel as heroic and unstoppable. Brueggemann says of unsolicited testimony something that is true of Judges 5: "much is stated extravagantly, inordinately, hyperbolically. In its witness, Israel delights to make a bold presentation in front of the watching nations."[28] Here we learn more of the ancient power of God, the One who marched from Seir and caused cosmic disruption with every holy footfall. We learn, in exquisite poetic detail, of the prosperity and luxury that Israelite peasants and nobility alike enjoyed under the judgeship of Deborah (5:7, 10). We learn that the heavenly luminaries themselves were mustered on the side of Israel, and the foe was swept away by the Kishon waters (an echo of Egypt's defeat at the Red Sea).

But this testimony also reveals matters that are dangerous: disputes, self-interest, and fear are rife among the tribes of Israel. Finally, Jael's exploit is hymned—it would seem that the divisions within Israel were not fatal, and our anxiety subsides. The poem closes with the taunting—or is it haunting?—image of Sisera's mother at the window reassuring herself that her son is delayed only because he is helping himself to spoils and female captives. The poem is epic, majestic . . . and unsettling. For here Israel does not narrate itself as the unified holy-war group that we saw in Judges 4. Israel is fractured, divided, and deeply at risk. The opening of the poem highlights the crucial role of those who "offer themselves willingly" for the cause (5:2, 9); this shows up all the more clearly that the refusal of four tribes to fight puts the entire Israelite group in danger. One wonders whether the stars and the Kishon had

27. J. Clinton McCann, *Judges*, Interpretation (Louisville, KY: John Knox Press, 2002), 49.

28. Brueggemann, *Theology of the Old Testament: Testimony, Dispute, Advocacy* (Minneapolis: Fortress Press, 1997), 408.

to fight because Israel's forces were not enough. If Sisera's mother waits for a victor who will never come, perhaps Israel watches, too, as the vulnerability of its own victors is subtly revealed. In Judges 4–5, we have two distinct testimonies, each "uttering" its own portrait of God and, in more contestatory terms, its own portrait of Israel.

Now, how might we read Judges 4–5 in light of Bakhtin's attention to dialogical double-voicing? Many possibilities offer themselves; here we will limit ourselves to two issues. First, we might inquire into the rhetorical effect of the Deuteronomistic framing of Judges 4. The pattern in Judges plays out over and over again: Israel sins, the Lord gives Israel into the hand of an enemy, Israel cries out, and the Lord raises up a deliverer (see Judg. 2:11–22). This overarching pattern locks the heroic narrative of Judges 4 into an unyielding Deuteronomistic structure that limns increasing moral decay in Israel as the book of Judges unfolds. The Israelites may have been redeemed, but their relief from oppression will be only fleeting; of that we can be sure. The key word "hand" (Hebrew *yad*) links all of the actors here: the cruel hand of Jabin (4:2), the trembling hand of Barak (4:7, 14), the mighty hand of Jael (4:9, 21), and the ruthless hand of the Israelites pressing Jabin into submission (4:24). Each time "hand" is uttered, it becomes more than it had been; the hands of enemy Jabin, Israelite commander Barak, and unexpected ally Jael blur into one another, complicating the destinies of the characters and revealing the controlling hand of God behind it all. By the end of the story, no one is what he or she had seemed: Jabin, brutal oppressor for twenty years, is rendered powerless and destroyed; Barak, commander of thousands, has missed the most decisive battle moment and scurries breathlessly into the scene only at the denouement; Jael, mistaken for a helpless woman and friend of the Canaanites, shows herself to be a treacherous and invincible warrior on the side of Israel. They all play their unexpected roles in a monologue directed by a God who is in complete control of history and who metes out punishment and rescue as suits the divine purpose. The ostensible openness and shifting expectations mediated by the storytelling in Judges 4 are clad, in fact, in a theological framework of iron.

A second issue of Bakhtinian dialogism arises with the tensive interplay of epic form and anxious content in Judges 5. The glorious song framed by ancient bards evokes the powerful tradition of God as Divine Warrior striding to battle through the southern wilderness (cf. Ps. 68). Mountains quake before this God; stars and river fight at God's behest; the people of God march steadfastly to battle. The epic is like a brilliant shield of holy-war discourse protecting the vulnerable side of the culture. But another diction whispers through almost imperceptible fissures in this shield, and we can hear fear. Reuben was conflicted; Gilead did not come; Dan and Asher refused to be mustered for war; "Meroz" (a now-unknown village) declined as well, earning a bitter curse from none other than the angel of the Lord. The epic nature of the poem begins to seem overcompensatory. Clearly, those four tribes and Meroz felt no need to submit to the power of God! Holy war tradition stipulates that when God is fighting on behalf of Israel, Israel's ranks may be purposefully thinned with no deleterious effect on the outcome of the battle. So why the concern about which tribes participated? Why the rhetorical questions imploring the tribes of Reuben and Dan to explain themselves (5:16–17)? Does this epic people not, in fact, trust its epic God? The monologue of victory has become fragile. The song is still glorious, but the voice of the Heldentenor wavers and cracks in unexpected places.

Multiple traditions abound in Scripture. This is crystal clear in the Pentateuch, with its distinct Priestly, Deuteronomic, and other traditions and language. We see this as well in Judges 4–5; we see it in doublets and narrative discontinuities in the stories about Saul and David; and we see it in the diverse accounts of the life of Jesus in the four Gospels. We may rejoice in the rich music that they sing together; we may delight in harmonies and dissonances alike. The readerly experience of being unsettled by conflicting Scripture traditions is real, and it is important to acknowledge that. But we should examine why we have a need for monologue, for monolithic truth, when the reality of the journey is so much more complex. When we encounter contestatory moments in our sacred texts, we may struggle through to a fuller and more complete picture of the God who far surpasses any one human language, set of metaphors, or particular storytelling mode. We may reap spiritual fruit from considering the uniqueness of each witness and the importance of the ways in which they speak differently about God and Israel. And we may commit ourselves to hearing and honoring each voice on its own terms as a mandate of Christian hermeneutical ethics. This is wrestling that matters—and the rewards are great indeed.

FOR FURTHER READING

Fretheim, Terence E. *The Pentateuch*. Interpreting Biblical Texts. Nashville: Abingdon Press, 1996.

Nicholson, E. W. *The Pentateuch in the Twentieth Century: The Legacy of Julius Wellhausen*. Oxford: Clarendon Press, 1998.

van Wijk-Bos, Johanna W. H. *Making Wise the Simple: The Torah in Christian Faith and Practice*. Grand Rapids: Wm. B. Eerdmans Pub. Co., 2005.

Whybray, R. N. *The Making of the Pentateuch: A Methodological Study*. Sheffield: JSOT Press, 1987.

Yee, Gale A., ed. *Judges and Method: New Approaches in Biblical Studies*. 2nd ed. Minneapolis: Fortress Press, 2007.

3

Foundational Narratives, History, and Voices from the Margins

The New Testament scholar had reached the end of his rope. He was happy to give an evening presentation occasionally at this charming Congregational church nestled in the lush green hillside of a town forty-five minutes from his theological school. The church paid visiting speakers well, the congregation was avidly interested in adult education about Scripture, and the discussions were never boring. But this particular evening, one middle-aged parishioner was becoming a little too insistent with his questions about historical events in the Bible. He had asked why the scholar was using terms such as "post-Easter narrative" and "communal memory" to talk about Jesus' resurrection. "The community 'remembered' this in a certain way?" the man mused, looking puzzled. "But . . . it did happen as the Bible says, right? I mean, all the Gospels say Jesus rose from the dead." The scholar hemmed and hawed. He was not here to challenge anyone's faith. It was late, and he was tired. Groping for language to characterize the composition of the Gospels accurately while not giving offense, he offered something about resurrection "traditions" having been elaborated by later communities as part of their own identity formation as Christians in a Hellenistic world. But the parishioner just wouldn't let it go. "So are you saying that these 'post-Easter' communities just made up the resurrection? Is the Bible wrong? Are you saying the resurrection isn't true?" Finally the biblical scholar had had enough. "It didn't happen," he snapped. "Get over it."

This vignette illustrates the clash of two different paradigms for understanding the relationship of history and text. The parishioner was assuming that a reliable and fairly transparent connection obtained between historical events and the Scripture texts that related them: the Bible accurately "mirrored" what had actually happened in first-century Palestine. Even if communities did shape texts according to their own biases and needs, still, something as important as Jesus' resurrection had to be fundamentally true. Otherwise, Scripture could not be considered trustworthy. The scholar, on the other hand, had been trained to think about texts as cultural productions that aim to persuade their audiences of particular viewpoints. He knew well the theological and political bent of each of the four Gospels and had expert knowledge of the influences on those texts from Second Temple Judaism and the various Hellenistic philosophical schools that were prominent at the time. He was a Christian believer, sure, but he was also a pragmatist. The truth of an event could not be adjudicated by looking at any text in isolation. The scholar relied on both his common sense and his post-Enlightenment understanding of the scientific world. Because he did not believe that miracles were possible, he felt confident in his position that the New Testament accounts of the resurrection were different versions of an ideologically shaped myth of Christian origins.

Who is right? Both of them are.

The parishioner was inquiring into the lived experience that generated the written articulations of Jesus' resurrection in the Gospels. He was conceiving of the New Testament texts as responses to real events that catalyzed awe, praise, reflection, and then proclamation in the believers of ancient times. If something like a resurrection hadn't happened—at least on some level, in some way—then we would not have written texts lying before us that make so much of it theologically. Does that sound naive to your ears? Not to mine. When something important happens—whether it be a personal moment of challenge that a memoirist wants to record privately in her journal or a public event that catalyzes a frenzy of blogging, the filing of dozens of newspaper reports, and novelistic and poetic reflections—texts are generated by those who want to engage the event that has happened. It's not that events "cause" writing, to be sure. And things "happen" in our imaginations, too (I mean that in the best possible sense: the inspiration for a poem can happen in our imagination, and new insight into a relationship or an ethics problem unfolds in our imagination too). Yet there is no question that cultural production is spurred and energized by lived experience. The parishioner was basing his question on *that* dimension of the relationship between text and history, and it is a perfectly intelligent way to think. It also happens to be my own view. I do not believe that all of Christian tradition rests on a metaphor (Christ's "resurrection") that was created contrary to fact. Rationalist objections to the incarnation and resurrection of our Lord are not particularly compelling, to my mind, once we see that the Enlightenment's valorizing of rationalism is itself limited and culturally conditioned.

But writing is also a process freighted with the desires and anxieties, the cultural biases and ignorance, and the political agendas of those who write.

There is no necessary or transparent relationship between what is "lived" or imagined or observed and the creative ways in which an author's text might configure that experience. The professor in our vignette knew well that a host of factors probably influenced the shaping of the resurrection accounts in the Gospels. These would certainly include the ancient Christian communities' experience of profound transformation on a level that begged for articulation in terms of the miraculous; early Christian apologists' need to portray a publicly shamed and martyred teacher as a triumphant messiah in accordance with religious expectations then current in the environment of Roman imperial cults; and the sociopolitical need of followers of Jesus to create a cultural narrative that defended their integrity and authorized their unorthodox religious beliefs in the face of the prejudice, marginalization, and even persecution that they continued to suffer in their Greco-Roman milieu.[1]

BIAS IN REPRESENTATION

Consider the following example about bias in the cultural politics of archaeology, a discipline that has traditionally been seen—by historical positivists, at least—to operate through the rational application of the purportedly value-neutral scientific method. (That method is itself a product of Enlightenment-era values and priorities shaped by an academic elite working largely in Western Europe and North America.) This is an anecdote about a British explorer, Gertrude Caton-Thompson, working in the 1930s:

> Gertrude was given a grant from the British Association for the Advancement of Science to study stone ruins in British-controlled Zimbabwe. Her conclusions about their origins were as controversial as they were courageous, for she reported back that the Zimbabwe findings indicated the presence of a highly evolved and structured African society, entirely indigenous; they were *not* the product of white Mesopotamian or Greek influence, as prevailing opinion held. This stirred quite a debate in archaeological circles.[2]

What we see when we observe, say, historical events and the material traces left by sociopolitical dynamics, is thoroughly conditioned by our own norms, priorities, and preformed conclusions. We see largely what we expect

1. For an accessible discussion of traditions of kingship and messianic identity as these were applied to Jesus in the New Testament, see Adela Yarbro Collins and John J. Collins, *King and Messiah as Son of God: Divine, Human, and Angelic Messianic Figures in Biblical and Related Literature* (Grand Rapids: Wm. B. Eerdmans Pub. Co., 2008).

2. Jane Fletcher Geniesse, *Passionate Nomad: The Life of Freya Stark* (New York: Modern Library, 2001), 202, with original emphasis.

to see, and we can be shocked to learn that a reality is quite different from our perception of it. How societies represent things will depend heavily on the existence—or absence—of a cultural diction expansive and malleable enough to enable them to describe something new that may fall outside the realm of what they expect.

> "Historical evidence is not made up of pre-existing, objective facts; it is produced through a process of interpretation, and so it can always be reinterpreted in line with a particular theory—or simply explained away."
>
> —Neville Morley, *Theories, Models, and Concepts in Ancient History* (2004), 16

Now, I am convinced that reality exceeds our construals of it. I am just old-fashioned enough to affirm that a tree *does* make a sound if it falls in the forest and no one hears it. But I also know that any story or poem written about the tree falling would be shaped, perhaps dramatically, by the artistic goals and cultural idiosyncrasies and perceptions of the writer. And I am well aware that folks can easily make up stories about trees falling when no actual tree has fallen. How are historical events related, then, to the Scripture texts that narrate them? In what follows, we will consider this complex question as it has been fiercely debated in the guild of Old Testament studies. Each of us will have to decide which elements in these debates carry the most weight for us, given our intellectual and ethical commitments, our position within a particular ecclesial tradition, and what our own lived experience tells us.

Thinking back to our vignette, and at the risk of irking those who side with the parishioner and those who side with the professor alike, I offer this: the biblical historicity issue is not a simple question of whether something did or didn't happen. It is a matter of how we negotiate multiple kinds of evidences that are revelatory of and shaped by intellectual assumptions, faith claims, and cultural norms grounded in the lived experiences of ancient communities. Moving forward into the discussion, I share my governing convictions on this subject:

- Memory is powerful.
- Creativity and bias are intrinsic to cultural production.
- God is real.

Our approach as believers to sacred texts that speak of generative, world-changing historical events should take account of all of these dimensions of biblical testimony. Memories of many different kinds exert powerful influences on Scripture traditions. Any cultural production (whether it be a text, a ritual, an engraving, an oil lamp, or something else) will inevitably be marked by both creativity and bias. And no matter what aspects of your intellectual convictions or spiritual beliefs may be challenged or deconstructed by what you learn, God is still real!

As we proceed, I invite you to reflect on and articulate the touchstone principles that guide your own understanding of ancient history and its implications for faith. Moments of surprise and even dismay are intrinsic to the learning process, no less than are moments of curiosity and the thrill of discovery. Preparing for and staying present to the destabilizing moments will help ensure that they become valuable resources on which we can draw as we continue to learn.

THE MYSTERY OF BIBLICAL HISTORY

If you are currently in seminary or had some theological study (whether in college or graduate school), you probably have at least one history of ancient Israel on your desk. Introductory textbooks about the history of ancient Israel and Judah tend to be sanguine about the possibility of constructing a coherent metanarrative on their subject—after all, that is precisely the task such textbooks are designed to address. You may have worked with the classic John Bright textbook *A History of Israel*; or the erudite *A History of Ancient Israel and Judah* by J. Maxwell Miller and John H. Hayes; or the clear and accessible *The Old Testament: A Historical and Literary Introduction to the Hebrew Scriptures* by Michael D. Coogan; or perhaps the spirited volume by Iain Provan, V. Philips Long, and Tremper Longman III, *A Biblical History of Israel*.[3] Each of these volumes, in its own way and for understandable reasons, presents the historical project as eminently achievable and reasonably clear-cut.

But interpreters argue fiercely about a whole host of historical issues regarding biblical representations of ancient Israelite life, especially for the periods earlier than the divided monarchy. We cannot delve into all of the relevant issues here. Many balanced books—and a substantial number of polemical books—have been written on the historicity of the Bible. Tempers run high. Some of the nastiest disputes I've witnessed between scholars have happened at national guild meetings when a matter of ancient Israelite history was being discussed. The tone can turn less than charitable, too, in debates

3. John Bright, *A History of Israel*, 4th ed. (Louisville, KY: Westminster John Knox Press, 2000); J. Maxwell Miller and John H. Hayes, *A History of Ancient Israel and Judah*, 2nd ed. (Louisville, KY: Westminster John Knox Press, 2006); for Coogan, *Old Testament: A Historical and Literary Introduction*, see chap. 2, note 5; Iain Provan, V. Philips Long, and Tremper Longman III, *A Biblical History of Israel* (Louisville, KY: Westminster John Knox Press, 2003).

between "Bible-believing" laypeople and professional historians. Scholars find themselves continually having to defend themselves, as Roman Catholic scholar Mark S. Smith does below:

> Contrary to a view popular among some fundamentalists, biblical scholars are not evil people or misguided people trying to sabotage religious faith. On the contrary, many biblical scholars are intensely devoted to their religious traditions and to their God. The bigger problem that I see is what I would call the "idolatry of history." Many people devoted to the Bible as divine revelation share a major assumption with people who are critical of religious faith and devotion to the Bible . . . [namely], that the truth of the Bible stands or falls on whether the Bible is always historically true. . . . Whether one accepts or criticizes the Bible as historical truth, historical veracity is hardly the single biblical standard for truth. Instead, the Bible fundamentally proclaims the reality of God in human lives and the implications that flow from that reality.[4]

Part of the problem is, we may never have anywhere near all the data we might want in order to understand fully some of the time periods discussed in the Bible. The time of the patriarchs may remain forever shrouded in mystery: there are few significant archaeological remains from that period that we could reasonably expect to have survived the ravages of time, given the social structure of seminomadic pastoralists living and moving about in small clan groups. Definitive description of the period of the judges, too, eludes us. As one scholar wrote in 1999,

> It is becoming more and more unlikely that a consensus will develop among biblical scholars concerning the early history of Israel any time in the near future. If anything, there is a heightened rhetoric that in some instances obscures the real issues. This lack of consensus regarding premonarchic Israel can be seen in the very diverse reconstructions that employ the same basic data. As the field of biblical studies enters a new millennium, the only apparent consensus is that the Albrightian "conquest" model is invalidated.[5]

The extent and nature of the Babylonian exile and the return under Cyrus are debated in scholarly circles, as well. Among the problems that scholars tackle are the questions of the historical accuracy of the prophets' depictions of life in exilic Judah and Babylon and the degree to which the land of Judah was truly "empty" after Nebuchadnezzar's massive deportations of Judeans.

4. Mark S. Smith, *The Memoirs of God: History, Memory, and the Experience of the Divine in Ancient Israel* (Minneapolis: Fortress Press, 2004), 163–64.

5. K. Lawson Younger Jr., "Early Israel in Recent Biblical Scholarship," in *The Face of Old Testament Studies: A Survey of Contemporary Approaches*, ed. David W. Baker and Bill T. Arnold (Grand Rapids: Baker Academic, 1999), 176.

On these and other matters, the biblical traditions brim with details that beg for sophisticated analysis of political structures and textual ideologies, ethnographic and other demographic information, iconography and other artifacts of visual culture, and diverse kinds of anthropological data.

And then there are the genre questions. It's important to consider which kinds of material were intended as historiography and which were not, yet this is a distinction that some nonhistorians have never considered when they think about Scripture. Was the story of Jonah being swallowed by a great fish intended as historical reportage or as instructive fable? Many biblical scholars and others would choose the latter option, but there are ecclesial traditions that insist on the historical nature of all material in the Bible, effectively discounting the question of genre entirely.

> "What *is* historical in the biblical narratives? Speaking snakes, talking donkeys, prophet-containing great fish, millions of people leaving a country overnight, forty years of trekking in the wilderness without sandals wearing out? These are surely the stuff of legend. What then? An Israel which in turn destroyed Egyptian and Assyrian forces by no . . . means other than divine intervention? An Israel which was instrumental in the humiliation of all the empires, including the slaughter of more than 75,000 Persians (Esth. 9.5–14), and whose choral activities could be used to generate an 'ambush of YHWH' (2 Chron. 20; music as the continuation of war by other means)? Surely not! What is historical and what is ideological fiction in such stories? It is the sorting out of these factors which constitutes, for me, one of the central elements of 'the problem of the Bible and history.'"
>
> —Robert P. Carroll, "Madonna of Silences: Clio and the Bible" (1997), 90, with original emphasis

There are plenty of mysterious issues to tackle when we consider the Bible and history. But in many of those instances, our biblical texts do not necessarily present a starkly defined historical problem that is troubling to most Christian readers. So while those issues are well worth studying, we will not engage them here. Below, we will consider three issues that do regularly worry Christian believers and can be downright shocking to those who are new to the critical analysis of history: (1) the ways in which other ancient Near Eastern cultures have influenced the theological expressions of faith in the Hebrew Scriptures, something that bothers those who want biblical faith to be absolutely unique; (2) challenge to the historicity of the exodus and conquest traditions, which is worrisome to those who expect biblical traditions to be accurate in terms of modern historiography; and (3) debates concerning the historical stature and character of King David, which disturb those who would prefer to see David as a moral and spiritual paradigm for the contemporary believer.

INFLUENCES FROM OTHER ANCIENT NEAR EASTERN CULTURES

Much has been made of parallels between Old Testament traditions and traditions of surrounding cultures of the ancient Near East. Particularly important for our understanding of the writings of ancient Israel are the cultures of ancient Mesopotamia, Ugarit, and Egypt, with their rich deposits of literature, art, political and trade documents, and other material artifacts from the centuries before and concurrent with the time of formation of the biblical writings. Comparative studies drawing on linguistic and cultural connections between ancient Israel and its neighbors have flourished, beginning in earnest in the late nineteenth century and burgeoning at a particularly rapid rate since the 1928 discovery of a hitherto unknown Canaanite script on clay tablets near a place called Ras Shamra in Syria. Semitic philology (the study of the Hebrew language and related languages) relies heavily on comparative linguistics; that seems to be fairly nonthreatening even for believers who staunchly resist claims of other kinds of influence.

But what about the cross-influence of genres and motifs that are of fundamental importance to biblical texts? If the beloved story of baby Moses floating down the Nile in a basket made of bulrushes turns out to be a hackneyed motif that we can also see in the Sumerian story of baby Sargon of Akkad, how can we know for sure that the biblical stories about Moses are accurate?[6] How are we supposed to understand the Psalms' imagery of God riding on the clouds and controlling lightning and hail, given that these divine predicates are well known from earlier Canaanite mythology about the storm god Baal? If a mythopoetic tradition of combat among the gods is reflected in what God says in Job 38–41 about having confined the sea and subdued Leviathan, does this mean that traditions in our Bible were originally polytheistic?[7] If the revelation of the Torah on Sinai was God's unique gift to Israel, what do we make of the fact that the covenant treaty form underlying the Ten Commandments is similar to forms seen in ancient Hittite culture?

A good number of Jewish and Christian scholars have felt the need to defend the uniqueness of the Old Testament in the face of comparative ancient Near

6. For a discussion of the Sargon birth legend, see Mark W. Chavalas, ed., *The Ancient Near East: Historical Sources in Translation* (Oxford: Blackwell Pub., 2006), 22–25.

7. An accessible resource on this topic is Bernard F. Batto, *Slaying the Dragon: Mythmaking in the Biblical Tradition* (Louisville, KY: Westminster John Knox Press, 1992).

Eastern studies. Why? Because serious theological questions arise when influences from non-Israelite cultures are discerned in the sacred texts of Israel. If the Bible is the revealed Word of God given to a particular chosen people through inspired human intermediaries, what place can there be for profane human cultural influences in shaping that divine Word? What does it mean for the revelatory authority of, say, the flood story in Genesis that there are other flood stories in ancient cultures whose denizens worshiped deities other than the God of Israel? If these other cultures had some of the same literary forms and images earlier than ancient Israel did, and those other cultures worshiped false gods, does that compromise the truth of Israel's sacred traditions? Anxiety about these questions led to the establishment of criteria by which Israel's religion could be celebrated as unique and distinctive even while cross-cultural influences were being acknowledged in many subdisciplines of biblical studies. Mark Smith provides a handy summary of the sorts of points that were scored in ancient Israel's "defense" by those who worried about the implications of comparative work. Smith quotes a reactionary passage from Ulf Oldenburg to make the point:

> The more I studied pre-Israelite religion, the more I was amazed with its utter depravity and wickedness. Indeed, there was *nothing* in it to inspire the sublime faith of Yahweh. His coming is like the rising sun dispelling the darkness of Canaanite superstition.[8]

Smith goes on to describe the aggressive privileging of Israelite religion on many different counts in these comparative endeavors:

> Sometimes condemnation of the Canaanites took subtler form. For example, we may note the contrast drawn between the historical outlook of Israel and the nature and mythic religion of Canaan in the work of G. Ernest Wright and many others, or G. E. Mendenhall's later distinction between the covenant religion of Israel and the power religion of Canaanite polytheism. . . . To dramatize the contrastive approach, we may list the main categories:

Canaan	*Israel*
polytheistic	monotheistic
wicked/depraved	moral
natural (fertility)	historical
mythical	historical
magical	moral
power	covenantal

8. Ulf Oldenburg, *The Conflict between El and Ba'al in Canaanite Religion* (Leiden: E. J. Brill, 1969), xi, with original emphasis. Quoted in Mark S. Smith, *Untold Stories: The Bible and Ugaritic Studies in the Twentieth Century* (Peabody, MA: Hendrickson Publishers, 2001), 98.

> These oppositions all share modern values associated with modern Western religion, in particular the so-called "Judeo-Christian tradition" (itself a Christian ideological construct). Scholars have since criticized the weaknesses in the contrastive views, including the tendency of many who championed such contrasts to overlook the mythic elements in Israelite literature.[9]

Cultural bias and anxiety about influence, then, sometimes lead Jewish and Christian scholars to make into a despised "Other" the cultures and beliefs of surrounding groups in the ancient Near East.

Naturally, I cannot solve the influence problem for believers who continue to be disturbed by ancient Near Eastern parallels to biblical traditions. But I do suggest that in any learning process, it is important to sit with and reflect on feelings of friction and disquiet. Those feelings constitute valuable opportunities for clarifying what one thinks, exploring what one doubts, and discerning where one might be willing to be open to new information or a new way of framing a question. How do I negotiate the implications of ancient Near Eastern cross-cultural fertilization? Drawing on my three convictions articulated above, I would affirm these points:

> Memory is powerful and hence, Israel's memories of contact with ancient Canaanite, Mesopotamian, and Egyptian cultures will certainly have had important effects on the ways in which Israel frames its religious experience. This is all part of how God has worked to make God's holy Word visible and persuasive through the efforts of culturally situated and embodied human beings.
>
> Creativity and bias are inevitable in the cultural production of biblical texts, which, after all, point to a God who cannot be contained or sufficiently described by any human language, including the languages of Scripture. It is spiritually salutary to stay alert to ways in which our creative and vested testimony about God may invite us into new understanding or, alternatively, may become an obstacle to our fuller perception of God's truth.
>
> Our mighty and matchless God is real and continues to be worthy of praise. This is true whether or not Canaanite worshipers used cloud-rider imagery for a deity whom we do not believe to have actually existed, whether or not a flood story from another culture attributes salvation to another deity, and so on.

Now, these points may not suffice for you, especially if you belong to an ecclesial tradition that emphasizes scriptural inerrancy. In that case, I invite you to consider how you might best draw on the resources of your own tradition as you reflect on the significance of cross-cultural influence on the Bible.

9. Smith, *Untold Stories*, 98–99.

On the methodological side of things, comparativists can be overenthusiastic about interpreting parallels between ancient cultures as necessarily significant. Not infrequently, even today, we can see comparativists pointing to parallel themes or cultural norms as if the simple identification of them suffices for our interpretation of biblical texts. This happens in various subdisciplines within biblical studies. Philologists sometimes argue for a particularly difficult meaning of a rare Hebrew word on the basis of an apparent cognate in another language even if the contexts of the two literatures are utterly dissimilar otherwise. The parade example of overzealous comparative philological work has been Mitchell Dahood's exegesis of the Psalms in light of Ugaritic in his Anchor Bible commentaries, published between 1965 and 1970. But you can see simplistic appeals to cognate languages made more broadly, without any kind of sophisticated argumentation regarding the syntactical functions, rhetorical purposes, and other deeper semantic features of language use and dimensions of cross-cultural linguistic fertilization that might be relevant. We also see broad-brush appeals to motifs or practices from other ancient Near Eastern cultures without carefully delineated methodological controls for assessing actual influence or the absence of same in the biblical texts. Consider the dry caveat of Peter Ackroyd, an Old Testament scholar of an earlier generation, whose disciplined caution about overstating any comparative case remains exemplary. Writing in 1968, he said,

> It is, of course, true that the wealth of discoveries, particularly in the whole Near Eastern area during the last century or so, has demonstrated the many interconnections within the area. . . . But to imagine that points of similarity necessarily point to direct influence or interconnection is also hazardous. . . . To see a golden figure from Ur as a "ram caught in a thicket" because of Genesis 22.13, in spite of the fact that it appears more probable that the figure represents a goat, and that so far from being caught in a thicket, it may more probably be regarded as eating the twigs of a bush, is, understandably, tempting enough, but results in not a little confusion of thought.[10]

Comparative work will continue to be invaluable for assessing the situatedness of ancient Israelite literature in its cultural milieus over the centuries during which biblical traditions achieved written expression. But methodological sophistication must be demanded when the rough cross-cultural data are applied to biblical texts. Comparative work cannot stand by itself, underanalyzed, as anything close to a sufficient guide to the theological, sociopolitical, and cultural richness of biblical traditions as we now have them in Scripture. The narrative and poetic artistry, rhetorical structures, genre-encoded cultural norms, and theological force of the varied traditions we see

10. Peter Ackroyd, *Exile and Restoration* (Philadelphia: Westminster Press, 1968), 8–11.

in the Hebrew Scriptures certainly owe a debt to surrounding cultures, but they are much more than can be accounted for by that debt.

> "We should not conclude, of course, that there were no differences at all between Israel and Judah and their neighbors. The existence of a 'Yahweh-alone' movement, even as a minority, would prove enormously important over time, and some such sentiment may have been quite old. . . . Hebrew prophecy was significantly different from that of other Near Eastern peoples in the degree of its concern with moral and social issues. The same might be said of biblical law. Moreover, there seems to have been an exclusivistic strain in Yahwistic religion from very early times, even if it did not always dominate."
>
> —John J. Collins, *The Bible after Babel* (2005), 127–28

As you continue to reflect on cross-cultural influences in the Bible, you may want to incorporate your thoughts on these two theological subjects, among others: first, what the incarnation may mean theologically for the sanctifying of all culture; and second, the idea that all dictions and languages (including metaphors and artistic images and music) are gifts from God for communication of the Holy.

THE POTENTIAL OF INCARNATIONAL THEOLOGY

First, imagine the enormous potential of incarnational theology to address these issues. The incarnation of our Lord into the messiness and beauty and brokenness of human life invites us to meditate on the power of God to be known in that life, and more, to transform all that is limited, inadequate, particular, and local. The category of "limited, inadequate, particular, and local" would include not only the flawed perceptions of the nonbelievers who rejected Jesus' teachings, but also the ironic and sometimes egregious misunderstandings of Jesus' own disciples that are retailed throughout the Gospels. Incarnational theology can help us to honor the particularity of first-century and twenty-first-century spiritualities alike. We can understand both the power and the limitations of witness—whether situated in ancient Palestine or in New Haven in 2010 or wherever you are right now as you read this—without confusing human spiritual understanding with the actual reality of the God whom we worship.

Incarnational theology invites us into places of challenge or joy about the ways in which local social norms and customs can blind us to the Holy (challenge!) or, conversely, can help us to perceive the Holy better (joy!). Canaanite religion is not outside the power of our God to redeem. The fact that many cultures tell ancient stories about a catastrophic deluge can deepen our eagerness to hear what *our* sacred Scriptures have to say about a God who was known through saving action in the flood. In all this, wrestle with your theological traditions as well as with Scripture, and trust that your lifelong learning process is superintended by the Holy Spirit.

DIVERSE CULTURAL EXPRESSIONS AS DIVINE GIFT

Second, we may consider diverse cultural expressions as a gift of God. Think of the appropriation of ancient Near Eastern treaty formulas in the Ten Commandments as a gift that helped to make those luminous imperatives intelligible to the ancient communities who heard them first. If Israel's liturgical poems, the Psalms, show traces of some very old imagery that had once belonged to the cult of the Canaanite god Baal—well, ponder what it might mean to have Storm God and Divine Warrior imagery predicated of a God whom Christians know to be Love. What does the power of the Divine Warrior motif mean for a God who calls us to servanthood (Matt. 23:11–12) and the daily sacrifice of self for others (Matt. 16:24–25; Mark 8:34–35; Luke 9:23–24)? You might reflect on the Beatitudes here: "The meek . . . will inherit the earth" (Matt. 5:5) takes on a new depth and beauty when we acknowledge that the meek are none other than disciples of a God whose "lightnings light up the world" (Ps. 97:4).

Or consider potential theological effects of the God of love being imaged in the dramatic language of theophany complete with earthquakes and tumultuous seas. God's love then becomes not just the kindness of a sweet friend or the gentle touch of a healer, but also the fierce compassion of One who could obliterate the world but chooses to die on the cross for it instead. Sheer gift!

Your own theology of the incarnation and your understanding of diverse cultural expressions of the sacred may lead you in different directions than these. That's fine. Just seek to articulate a theological framework that makes sense to you as you engage and interrogate this material. Use the resources of your faith tradition to reflect on the significance of everything that you learn about God's holy Word, including whatever fascinating information you glean about ancient Near Eastern cultural practices, parallels in extrabiblical literatures, ways in which the Israelites' and Judeans' understanding of God changed over time, and so on. Anything that is true can never threaten the God who is Truth.

DEBATES ABOUT THE HISTORICITY OF EXODUS AND CONQUEST TRADITIONS

The archaeological record that we have been able to uncover so far does not support the theory that a huge multitude of Israelites swept into Canaan from Egypt all at once. We do not see the drastic changes in material culture (sudden differences in the design of pottery and the like) that we would expect if a large group of cultural outsiders had arrived suddenly in Canaan, importing their foreign ways of working with ceramics, the decorative arts, and other materials. There are reliable hints in Hebrew Bible traditions about ancient contact with Egypt, to be sure. We know that Semitic rulers called the Hyksos came to power in Egypt briefly in the second millennium BCE, that the name of Moses looks Egyptian, and that the book of Exodus shows some (imperfect) knowledge of Egyptian dynastic rule, Egyptian words, and local geography. But in terms of the formation of an ethnically distinct and unified group called "Israel," the archaeological evidence—still debated, of course—seems to point more in the direction of a complex combination of factors over a longer period of time. These factors probably included some immigration from outside of Palestine, but also involved an internal movement from seminomadism to sedentarization and the strengthening of symbiotic relationships between pastoralists and other Canaanites, yielding the gradual solidifying of communal identity among various elements that likely included both indigenous Canaanites and outsiders. A further point is that pastoralist groups sometimes move and shift among activities of agriculture and herding, such that we ought not presume a kind of rigid stratification of function in the various groups that were interacting in ancient Palestine in any case.[11]

This complex picture of the emergence of ancient Israel makes good sense to me. But it does not accord well with the accounts in Exodus and Joshua. (It works a little better with the picture we see in the book of Judges.) The discrepancies between extrabiblical evidence and biblical representations pose a serious theological problem for those who cherish Scripture as authoritative, since many of us want to assume some reliable level of accuracy or authenticity in whatever we deem to have authority. The book of Exodus claims that God liberated the Israelites from Egyptian bondage through a series of signs and wonders, subduing the Egyptian oppressors and clearing the way for Moses to lead his people to the land of Canaan. The book of Joshua claims that a massive invading force of Israelites had to engage in warfare many times with indigenous Canaanite groups in order to dispossess them of their land and

11. Lester L. Grabbe, *Ancient Israel: What Do We Know and How Do We Know It?* (New York: T&T Clark, 2007), 102–3.

other holdings in fulfillment of God's promise to Israel, and Joshua claims further that God fought on the side of Israel. That story of divine liberation and conquest is absolutely foundational for Israelite identity as that is expressed in the Pentateuch, a good number of psalms, and some prophetic passages as well. If the exodus and conquest did not happen historically—even if we were to concede that the whole narrative is a powerful metaphor for redemption or a compelling mythical story intended to bolster the Israelites' trust in God—then for many readers, the truthfulness of Scripture is cast into doubt. And there are important ethical implications if we take away the real-life historical grounding of these events. If real people were not liberated from actual slavery, then at least some of us—me included—will not be so interested in the alternative: a claim that God is only "metaphorically" the One who led Israel out of Egypt.

> "We do not require 'positive grounds' for taking the biblical testimony about Israel's past seriously. We require positive grounds, rather, for *not* doing so. Only by embracing such epistemological openness to testimony, biblical and otherwise, can we avoid remaking the past entirely in our own image—can we avoid submitting to the delusion that we already 'know' about reality and to the consequent mistake of trying to impose that 'knowledge' on everything that questions it."
>
> —Iain Provan, V. Phillips Long, and Tremper Longman III,
> *A Biblical History of Israel* (2003), 74

Remember our vignette at the beginning of this chapter ("It didn't happen. Get over it")? Arguments about the exodus, too, are sometimes simplified to reductionist levels on both sides. "Maximalist" scholars such as Tremper Longman, Kenneth Kitchen, and James Hoffmeier offer robust defenses of orthodox biblical history, arguing that unless evidence concretely disproves the biblical account, the Bible's historical veracity should be allowed to stand. They are not wrong when they object that frequently the more skeptical scholars ("minimalists") argue from lack of evidence rather than from positive disconfirmation. But even conceding that, we see that many other scholars find historical evidence in the biblical accounts to be implausible to varying degrees. Joseph Blenkinsopp notes that numbers in the Bible are "either of the stereotypical kind or greatly exaggerated."[12] He says further, "The Pentateuchal narrative reveals a distinctive feature in the frequent occurrence of precise dates. . . . These chronological markers are undoubtedly

12. Blenkinsopp, *Pentateuch*, 38.

fictive."[13] Do fictitious dates and impossibly high numbers in biblical texts mean that the Bible "is not true"? This is a complex issue, because the question of how sacred texts are or are not "true" is itself complex. Numbers can signify quite different things in different cultures. Further, standards of accuracy or truth are also variable, calibrated to different measures depending on cultural norms. It is well known that many numbers have symbolic meanings in ancient Semitic (and other) cultures: the numerals seven, twelve, and forty, for example, can connote sacredness or completeness as well as serving to number particular things. The question of "exactly what happened" in ancient history cannot be easily quantified with any purely rationalist approach to ancient literature. Indeed, rationalism itself is fraught with unexplained and imperfect assumptions. One must become versed in the norms and expectations of ancient literature in order to understand how it means to represent what is true.

> "Archaeology does not, and cannot, claim to know all about the place it excavates, nor the people who lived there. . . . Archaeology *does not* prove the Bible to be 'true' or 'false.' It *does* provide, at times, strikingly helpful evidence for customs and practices mentioned in the Bible of which we had no previous examples. It can support the accuracy of Old Testament writers as observers of the daily life of their times. . . . But the literary and religious affirmations of Old Testament faith are not open to being believed because archaeology can support them. Never shall we find the truth about Abraham and Jacob from archaeological remains."
>
> —Lawrence Boadt, *Reading the Old Testament: An Introduction* (1984), 67–68

Minimalists argue that the exodus simply "didn't happen," period; these texts are the ideological productions of later generations of Israelite scribes who were using their construction of stories of origin toward various social and political ends. Maximalists argue that the Bible is more or less correct, at least in the big picture if not in every single detail. At Society of Biblical Literature annual meetings and in publications, the two sides tend to treat each other with thinly veiled hostility, if not outright derision. To evoke the broad contours of the arguments for you, I will bring points from maximalist scholars Kenneth Kitchen, Iain Provan with V. Phillips Long and Tremper Longman, and Richard Hess into dialogue with points from minimalist scholars Thomas Thompson, Philip Davies, and Keith Whitelam. I acknowledge

13. Ibid., 47.

that the labels "maximalist" and "minimalist" may not be the most refined of terms, but here they can serve as a helpful shorthand to signal whether the position taken is one that defends the biblical account (maximalist) or treats that account with skepticism (minimalist).

Minimalist	**Maximalist**
"The population of the central hills expanded during the course of Iron I. Along the steppelands and the desert fringe and in the central range, where herding was a dominant factor, the population doubled in size. . . . The highlanders seem clearly to have come from people displaced from the lowlands. It is unlikely that large numbers of nomadic pastoralists would have entered this region. . . .The initial pressure of the drought would have encouraged shepherds to move away from the steppe and into the better-watered highlands. The return to a better climate around 1050 BCE would likewise have supported a shift to agriculture." (Thompson, *The Mythic Past*, 159–61)	"That there *was* an entry by the Israelites into Canaan from outside is indicated clearly by the demographic situation revealed by modern archaeological surveys, revealing a whole rash of fresh, new, small settlements. In the 150 years circa 1150–1000, the population seems to have doubled, but in less than half that time, circa 1210–1150, it at least quintupled! A theoretical ongoing orgy of procreation for two generations can be dismissed as fantasy; the only answer is that numbers suddenly shot up because additional people came in." (Kitchen, *On the Reliability of the Old Testament*, 239)
"History is not 'the past' (except in a loose, idiomatic sense). It is not even 'what we happen to know about the past': it is 'what we choose to narrate about the past.' History is 'the past as meaningful,' and its meaning is created (*not* 'interpreted') by means of narrative. Narrative *generates* 'history' by means of the artificial selection, not only of a particular subject, time and place out of the past (as if any part of the past could be isolated in this way from everything else) but also by the unavoidable circumstance that we only know a fraction of the past anyway—and even that we cannot comprehend." (Davies, "Biblical Israel in the Ninth Century?" 49)	"The thirteenth-century destructions of Canaanite cities cannot be so neatly correlated with Israelite invaders as was once thought. They are simply too widely separated in time to have been the result of a single, even protracted campaign. Today, most scholars regard Albright's conquest model as a failure, which is not surprising since, as L. Younger observes, 'the [conquest] model was doomed from the beginning because of its literal, simplistic reading of Joshua.' It might be more accurate to speak of a simplistic *mis*reading of Joshua, for the conquest model assumes massive destruction of *property* as well as population, whereas the book of Joshua suggests no such thing. . . . Only three cities—Jericho, Ai, and Hazor—are said to have been burned. That only these three are mentioned does not imply that others *might not* have been burned, but

Minimalist	Maximalist
	it underscores the wrongheadedness of insisting that widespread city destructions should be attested archaeologically." (Provan, Long, and Longman, *A Biblical History of Israel*, 140)
"Grand-scale teleological histories became the norm within biblical studies despite the rise of modern, so-called scientific historiography. . . .The evolutionary notions that underpin such narratives—the triumph of the Israelite state over deficient Canaanite petty city-states or Israelite monotheism replacing the debauched religion of the Canaanites—are not fossilized relics of past scholarship but continue to exert a hold over current discussions concerning the David and Solomonic monarchy, notions of centralization, and the textualization of time." (Whitelam, "Setting the Scene," in *Understanding the History of Ancient Israel*, ed. Williamson, 18–19)	"The picture that emerges is of a group of West Semitic clans (collectively called 'Israel') that fled from Egypt under a leader who had spent time in Sinai after an Egyptian court upbringing and education. These factors were crucial in his ability to lead the group through the Sinai terrain; for marshaling the skills of the craftsmen in the group to build a traditional Semitic 'tabernacle' shrine, using Egyptian technology and motifs; and for formulating a foundation document ('covenant') making a nascent 'nation community' out of his clans, using—again—a suitable model learned in his court days." (Kitchen, *On the Reliability of the Old Testament*, 306)
"That the Old Testament is no longer believable as history offers really no difficulty to theology. It is after all very old. . . . It is not necessary either to deny the tradition or to baptize it. It is only important not to lie about our past. Theology is not—or at least should not be—confined to blind searches for a truth that doesn't and never did exist." (Thompson, *The Mythic Past*, 386)	"The escape of Israelite slaves from Egypt, together with the defeat of the Egyptian army at the Red (traditionally Reed) Sea, represents the single most significant theological event in Israel's memory. . . . That the exodus reflects a historical event, however large or small, is suggested both by the details of the narrative that set well in the context of Egypt of the thirteenth century BC, and by the generally recognized oddity of the account as a foundation story of a people's history. If there had been no oppression and no exodus, why would any Israelite author invent such an origin for her/his people? If Israel was indigenous to Canaan and never came from Egypt, how did this story come to form the beginning of this nation's epic?" (Hess, *Israelite Religions*, 154)
"As a result of recent archaeological work, biblical archaeology is now dead among professional archaeologists. It	"Prejudice against biblical testimony because of its ideological or theological orientation is, of course, commonly

Minimalist	Maximalist
lives on in the pages of *Biblical Archaeology Review* and in the fundamentalist community that insists that archaeology can only ever prove the Bible right and never disprove it." (Davies, *Memories of Ancient Israel*, 65)	found throughout modern writing on the history of Israel. . . . A basic presupposition of critical historical study at least since the Enlightenment has been that skepticism is the appropriate stance to adopt in relation to texts whose primary aim is to deliver a religious message." (Provan, Long, and Longman, *A Biblical History of Israel*, 62)

It is clear that historians of ancient Palestine disagree sharply over what constitutes appropriate use of the biblical narratives in historical discussions, how material evidence such as increased settlement in the hill country or the lack of a clearly demarcated ceramic style is to be explained, and what is at stake in the ideological underpinnings of opponents' arguments. While tempers flare in these debates and some remarks made—even in print—are inflammatory in the extreme, there are some balanced voices in the scholarly discussion. Thomas B. Dozeman points toward a way out of this impasse. Drawing on the work of Konrad Schmid, he highlights differences between the ancestral material and the Moses/Exodus material as follows. The ancestral stories (the tales of Abraham, Isaac, and Jacob, along with their families) show the Israelites as indigenous to Canaan, inclusive in their relationships with other peoples, and peaceful. By contrast, the Moses/Exodus narrative shows the Israelites as outsiders to Canaan, exclusionary in their relations with other peoples, and focused on holy war and conquest. Speaking of the clear disjuncture between the ancestral traditions and the exodus story, Dozeman writes:

> The past models for interpreting the Pentateuch have tended to harmonize the two traditions into one story of salvation history. . . . The hypothesis of the late formation of two origin traditions provides a new way of reading the canonical Pentateuch as two competing ideologies of land possession, one exclusive and violent and the other inclusive and peaceful. . . . A new reading of the Pentateuch as the juxtaposition of two competing origin traditions may provide a way to loosen the stranglehold that the ideology of holy war has had on contemporary appropriations of the Pentateuch.[14]

Dozeman helps us to recognize that "the biblical account" is not any one monolithic thing. As with our exploration of the multiple voices in the

14. Thomas B. Dozeman, "The Commission of Moses and the Book of Genesis," in *A Farewell to the Yahwist? The Composition of the Pentateuch in Recent European Interpretation*, ed. Thomas B. Dozeman and Konrad Schmid (Leiden: E. J. Brill; Boston: Society of Biblical Literature, 2006), 129.

Pentateuch, so too here we may listen more attentively to Scripture and discern testimony and countertestimony. In this case, we encounter distinct cultural memories of both pastoralism and conquest—both peaceful indigenous habitation and forcible intrusion marked by sustained conflict.

In my view, it is a deeply faithful way of reading to honor disjunctures and moments of friction that we perceive between different stories of Israel's origin preserved in our Bible. Any dogged concern to force these richly diverse traditions into one monolithic witness comes from outside of Scripture. Rather than suppressing our anxiety at a richly complicated set of testimonies, we can choose to be courageous readers who attend to points of cultural conflict—yes, even in our sacred writings—and embrace them as meaningful teaching moments. In the case of ancient Israelite origin traditions that are at odds with one another, we can listen for the many dimensions of truth that textured the lives of the ancient Israelite communities (plural) who sought to understand themselves and their God, early and late. We can listen for the claims and counterclaims of these multiple traditions without having to choose just one rigidly structured model according to only one kind of evidence.

> "Something called Israel existed in the Palestinian region about 1200 BCE, and it appears to have been a people. Exactly where this people lived, what/who constituted it, where it got its name and its relationship to the Israel of the Bible are all questions. . . . It seems that a variety of ethnic groups (Hittites, Hurrians, Jebusites, Girgashites, Amorites, Shasu [?] etc.), as well as social elements ('apiru, Shasu [?], pastoralists settling down, peasants fleeing the lowlands, etc.), settled the hill country on both sides of the Jordan in Iron I, if our written sources are anything to go by. . . . At some point a dominant ethnic consciousness came about in this region. Part of the reason might be by force: an 'Israelite' group might have conquered or otherwise taken over some other smaller groups and assimilated them (as suggested in Joshua and Judges)."
>
> —Lester L. Grabbe, *Ancient Israel* (2007), 119

DIMENSIONS OF TRUTH

Every community formed radically by faith experiences itself as an outsider to the secular culture (or other religious culture) in which it lives out its witness. Resistance to religious witness can indeed be violent. Conflict is all too real. Moreover, fantasies of conquering the Other—the outsider, the unbeliever, the heretic—may be seen as an inevitable dimension of the psychological and social experience of any group that relies on the notion of itself being set apart from its environment. This is no less true of Christian communities than of ancient Israel. Christian groups in many ages and cultures have worked to "conquer" the Other, whether those were identified as atheists, adherents of other faiths, or perceived heretics and misguided believers from within the Christian tradition. Christian history offers ample evidence of this, along a spectrum from the blood-soaked medieval Crusades to contemporary missional endeavors that work in a more nuanced way to proclaim an enculturated gospel. Thus the ancient cultural memory of a conflictual and violent Israelite penetration of Canaanite culture may be deemed true—in an *entirely real* sense—even if the archaeological evidence does not support a simplistic paradigm of a one-time, massive military invasion as the only event that happened in Israel's settlement of Palestine.

The gradual infiltration, peaceful settlement, and symbiotic models of the Israelite occupation of Canaan, too, surely capture dimensions of the truth of ancient Israelite experience. It is doubtless true that some Israelites came from Egyptian and Canaanite sociocultural contexts and peaceably infiltrated the highlands of Palestine. It is surely true that some Israelites experienced their journey from elsewhere, including Egypt, as arduous and their entry into a new community in the highlands of Palestine as fraught with conflict. Skirmishes between long-standing residents and new arrivals are the rule in many societies that experience change through immigration. Still others probably were Canaanites drawn to early Israelite communities, whether through intermarriage or religious conversion or simply through the bonds that can develop over time spent in close proximity, and these would have swelled the ranks of the Israelites from within their homeland.

I hope that the preceding discussion will have convinced you that "the exodus didn't happen" is not a satisfactory statement. The biblical narratives are far more complex than they are often given credit for, and the archaeological evidence, too, needs to be respected in all of its own complexity. As we continue to wrestle, we may hold fast to the fundamental theme of the exodus as theologically true, not despite but because of the incalculable complexities of life in community. What is that theme? It is that the God of Israel is a God of redemption who hears the cries of the oppressed. God's saving grace was true for all dimensions of Israel's lived experience. And I suspect, because I am a Christian who knows that God commands me to love the "enemy," that it was true for the Canaanites as well.

REDEEMED FOR OBEDIENCE

Even as we cheer God as liberator, we may realize that our wrestling is not yet over. We have seen Collins's important objection regarding the ethics of the exodus. The particularity of Israel in God's saving work presents another ongoing challenge to Christians. Though we have been grafted into Israel through the grace of God (Rom. 11), nevertheless we ought not commodify Israel's story, applying it happily as a metaphor to any situation in which a power imbalance is rectified, with no regard for the situatedness of that initial act of deliverance of *Israel*. That situatedness in the life of ancient Israel includes, specifically, the connection of the exodus to God's gift of the law and the divine imperative for Israel's brutal dispossession of the Canaanites. Jewish scholars such as Jon D. Levenson and Joel S. Baden remind us that the trajectory of deliverance doesn't just "include" law and conquest. One might fairly say that in its final form, the Pentateuch's overarching narratology drives inexorably toward and is centrally about law and conquest. On this view, the stories of the Pentateuch are all about the Israelites preparing—in many and various ways—for the moment when they arrive at Sinai and are given the torah. Further, the deliverance from Egypt cannot be read apart from the invasion of Canaan for which Israel's deliverance was the necessary preliminary step. Levenson writes:

> The Hebrew Bible does not conceive the exodus as a move from slavery to freedom, either freedom in the older, liberal sense of emancipation from external constraint for the purpose of self-determination, or freedom in the newer, Marxist sense of liberation from oppression and alienation for the purpose of equality, solidarity, and community. . . . For though God hears the groaning, crying, and moaning of the afflicted slaves, it is his memory of the still unfulfilled covenant with Abraham, Isaac, and Jacob that motivates him to send them the great deliverer Moses.[15]

Israel was freed in order to worship God according to the law. We may go further, of course. The covenant with the patriarchs included the granting not only of offspring but also of the territory of already-occupied Canaanite lands. So one challenge here is that if we Christians are to read the biblical account with an ear for "history," we will need to remember that the original deliverance was bound up with halakic regulations that Christians do not observe and an ideology of military conquest and genocide ("You must not let anything that breathes remain alive; you shall annihilate them"; Deut. 20:16–17) to which many of us would never subscribe today. That's history too.

Baden interprets narrative as entirely subsumed to law in the Pentateuch; he claims that there is no theological motivation at all to the original composition and ordering of the nonlegal material:

15. Jon D. Levenson, *The Hebrew Bible, the Old Testament, and Historical Criticism* (Louisville, KY: Westminster John Knox Press, 1993), 146, 153.

> The compilation of the Pentateuch was not a theological statement, nor was it meant to be taken as such. It was achieved . . . for the sole purpose of preserving the individual documents, precious to important segments of Israelite society, such that together they made up a single Israelite *law code*. . . . The narratives that surround the laws in each book [were] probably originally written only to provide the framework on the basis of which the laws were to be given historical and religious authority.[16]

Many readers of the Pentateuch will not want to go that far. Terence E. Fretheim interprets the fact that narrative and legal material are interwoven in the Torah from a perspective that privileges narrative theology. Consider the below nine points that Fretheim makes about reading law and narrative together in the Pentateuch:

1. Law is more clearly seen as another gift of God's graciousness for the sake of life and well-being rather than burden;
2. Obedience to the law is seen, not as a response to the law as law, but as a response to the story of all that God has done;
3. The story shows that the law is given to those already redeemed, as a way of doing justice to the relationship with God in which Israel already stands, not as a means to achieve salvation;
4. The law is more personally and relationally conceived when part of a story;
5. The law is not to be rigidly fixed, but moves with the story—new occasions teach new duties;
6. The story gives to the law a vocational character, a promoting and enhancing of the purposes of God for the creation decisively reclaimed by God's narrative deeds;
7. The shape that the law takes in Israel's life is to be measured by the shape of the narrative action of God (Be merciful, as God has been merciful);
8. The basic motivation for obeying the law is drawn from Israel's narrative experience with God rather than from abstract ethical argument or divine imperative;
9. That God is subject in both law and narrative provides for a continuity of divine purpose, grounded in the personal will of God.[17]

In different ways, Baden and Fretheim underline the point that we ought not consider the exodus and conquest stories in isolation, as if they were separated from the law that stands at the center of the Pentateuch. Israel was redeemed for obedience to the God who brought them out of Egypt. If that was indeed a feature of the historical events of the exodus and conquest, then that is a matter that Christian historicist readers need to take seriously, within

16. Baden, *J, E, and the Redaction of the Pentateuch*, 311.
17. Fretheim, *Pentateuch*, 124–25, with numbering added.

the Christian context. If we are grafted into Israel, then we too are redeemed for obedience (even if not for halakic obedience as such).

"History" does not include just discrete events. "History" also includes the intentions of artists and writers motivating the acts of cultural production that created texts (and paintings and ceramic jars and other artifacts). This point configures the category of history more broadly, which may be useful to you as you continue to wrestle with issues of historicity and textual representation. Is the exodus still meaningful if it is taken as a vague metaphor for liberation with no particularity whatsoever? Liberation in a general sense is fine and I'm all for it. But at a certain point, it seems to me that it is no longer "biblical" if we are employing the idea of exodus just as a general, watered-down metaphor. Do we read it as particular to Israel in an important and enduring way, even if we also dare to extrapolate to ourselves and to other oppressed peoples, including the Canaanites of ancient times and the "Canaanites" of today? Do we hear in that paradigmatic story of liberation the insistence that worship must be the response of those who have been freed? To what degree do *those* historical dimensions have a claim on us? Here, as with the other issues we have been addressing, I encourage you to engage the question in whatever dimensions make sense to you and to your ecclesial tradition. The wrestling may be uncomfortable at times, but it can only strengthen you as a reader and as a believer.

CONFLICTING ASSESSMENTS OF DAVID

In 2001 I attended a conference sponsored by the Association of Theological Schools for women in theological education. Gathered for three days in a Pittsburgh hotel were nearly a hundred talented, passionate women from seminaries and divinity schools all over the country. We talked about leadership strategies, obstacles to women's empowerment in the academy, pedagogy, and related issues. At one point the plenary group broke up into smaller workshops. I chose to attend a session led by an Old Testament professor from a well-known evangelical theological school. Her presentation was on biblical models for women's leadership. She mentioned Sarah and Ruth in passing, but the really memorable moment came when she revealed the biblical character she would be commending as the ideal model for our development of spiritual and pragmatic leadership skills. Who was this paradigm for women's leadership in the twenty-first century?

Samson. And she was completely serious.

Our dynamic presenter had chosen as our model a male character, which seemed to be somewhat of a missed opportunity given the good number of fascinating women characters in Scripture and given that the workshop was focused on women's agency. But more than that, she chose a biblical figure who is one of the most boorish and violent characters in ancient literature. Samson rudely orders his parents to procure a Philistine wife for him, despite their orthodox objections at the prospect of his marrying into an uncircumcised group of foreigners; he grotesquely eats honey out of the carcass of a lion; he is given to fits of enraged vengeance that put others in mortal danger and leave the bodies of many slaughtered in his wake; and he repeatedly indulges in sexual mixing with inappropriate Philistine women. I agree with those scholars who see in the book of Judges a rhetorical pattern of increasing violence and increasing ineffectiveness of the judges whom God raises up to deliver Israel. According to that pattern, Samson is meant to be understood as the least effective judge.[18] On my reading, his "heroism," while not entirely absent, is heavily ironized.

As our presenter's lauding of Samson went on—she found spiritually alluring his charisma and his strength when facing overwhelming odds—I realized that in her ecclesial tradition, believers were encouraged to make heroes out of biblical characters and try to live like them. This is not a standard feature of the Episcopal Church's approach to Bible study, at least not in the four Episcopal churches I've attended since childhood. But I know that for some readers of Scripture and some church traditions, it's important to be able to lionize biblical figures as heroes and heroines for believers to emulate. This hermeneutical move to valorize biblical figures as paradigms for living was so powerfully ingrained in our presenter that she could select the brutish and rapacious Samson as a role model for women theological educators with absolutely no sense of irony.

Whom else do Christian believers like to emulate in their spiritual lives? King David is probably the most glorified and lionized of all biblical figures in the church, after Jesus himself. Folks worry a little bit about the Bathsheba incident—oddly, their anxiety seems to center much more on the adultery aspect than on the part where David has a loyal, good man killed—but believers who love David tend to say that this just makes David "more human" and thus more accessible to us flawed sinners. Certainly many Scripture texts openly praise and commend David in hyperbolic terms, so David stands much readier to hand as a hero of the faith than does Samson, if we are looking for

18. Susan Niditch disagrees with those who claim that Samson is meant to be a thoroughly unsympathetic character. She writes, "Some scholars have treated Samson as a foolish dolt, an antihero, or a poor leader who makes the cries for a king in 1 Samuel 8 seem appropriate. . . . [But] Samson is a complex, epic-style hero who would be incomplete without flaws. His dangerous womanizing and his hubris, like his clever use of sayings and riddles and his Herculean acts of strength, all mark him as an Israelite version of an . . . action hero" (*Judges*, Old Testament Library [Louisville, KY: Westminster John Knox Press, 2008], 154).

heroes. But Scripture's witness to David is complex, and extrabiblical evidence again complicates the historical picture. Was David an ideal king, the beloved and powerful scion of a golden age in Israel's history, or was he a ruthless mercenary who collaborated with the Philistines and whose tenuous claim to the throne was bitterly contested by many who saw him as a usurper? Was David chosen by God to lead not only Israel and Judah but all the nations, who would eventually bow before the ineluctable power of his eternal and quasi-messianic dynasty (Isa. 55:1–5), or was he instead a minor chieftain of little account on the larger stage of ancient Near Eastern politics? Yes and yes. Scripture and extrabiblical evidence offer us all of these portraits of David.

Competing portraits of the moral stature of David may readily be seen in even a superficial reading of the biblical material, so I will not argue them at length here. Some biblical texts in the books of Samuel and (via superscriptions) in the Psalms give us a glorious David, handsome and charismatic, chosen and beloved of God, a gifted musician whose talents soothe the ranting Saul, a devout believer who lifts up exquisitely poetic praise to God. But other biblical texts show us a much darker portrait: we see a ruthless mercenary who is not above torturing his enemies, a traitor motivated by self-interest who, in the end, is loyal not to Israel but to the Philistines;[19] a narcissistic, callous, power-hungry monarch who plots to have a steadfast and devoted soldier killed so that David's adultery with the soldier's wife will not be revealed. And extrabiblical evidence gives us . . . well, very little about this David whose kingdom is hymned in the positive streams of biblical tradition as spectacular. We pause just briefly on the historicity question, long enough to note that there is a ninth-century BCE inscription recovered from Tel Dan that says "house of David," part of a victory boast of an Aramean king over other local rulers. Otherwise, many archaeologists argue that we lack the evidence for the kind of centralized state that the Bible postulates during the time of the united monarchy. Apart from the Tel Dan inscription, we lack evidence that other nations cared about David's dynastic power. Apparently the Davidic monarchy did not have much of an impact on nations who were not reading Israel's Scriptures.

An issue on which we can get more traction is the multidimensional portrayal of David's character in the Bible. Walter Brueggemann's *David's Truth in Israel's Imagination and Memory* (1985) can help us see the contested and pluriform refractions of traditions about David in the Hebrew Scriptures.

19. See Baruch Halpern, *David's Secret Demons: Messiah, Murderer, Traitor, King* (Grand Rapids: Wm. B. Eerdmans Pub. Co., 2001).

"Upon reading the Hebrew Bible, one would expect archaeology to prove the existence of a strong, mature state of David and Solomon with a large city in Jerusalem, dense urban settlement throughout the country, and formal inscriptions and art. . . . [Skeptics'] claims are that such a kingdom is not mentioned in any written sources outside the Bible; Jerusalem, its supposed capital, was either entirely unsettled or a small village during the tenth century; literacy is hardly known during this period; the population density was poor; there is no evidence for international trade, and more. . . . David's Jerusalem can be compared to a medieval Burg, surrounded by a medium-sized town, and yet it could well be the centre of a meaningful polity. . . . Short-lived achievements like those of David may be beyond what the tools of archaeology are capable of grasping."

—Amihai Mazar, "The Spade and the Text: The Interaction between Archaeology and Israelite History Relating to the Tenth–Ninth Centuries BCE" (2007), 146, 165

Brueggemann is interested in biblical constructions of David as the "engine for Israel's imagination and for Israel's public history."[20] He articulates four "modes of truth" about David, each connected to a particular social setting and need in the life of Israel. The David of the tribe is a cunning, charismatic renegade whose subversive example appeals to the poor, the dispossessed, and others not in power. He is the surprising outsider whose victory over Goliath cheers those who have been kept on the underside of Israel's material and political success. Another portrayal of David focuses on the interiority of this deeply flawed man who makes profound mistakes and yields to temptation, but who is yet capable of deep faith and resolve. This David reveals the pathos of the leader and of the human condition more broadly. A third David is articulated by the monarchical state as the ideal king whose loyalty to God is sure and whose dynasty will not fail. And a fourth portrait of David gives us the liturgically present, sublimely faithful composer-king who leads the worshiping community in hope toward the future that God has planned for Israel. While one might quibble with this or that detail of the social setting that Brueggemann proposes for each portrait, I would affirm that Brueggemann has listened carefully and well to the divergent characterizations of David that find expression in the Hebrew Scriptures.

20. Walter Brueggemann, *David's Truth in Israel's Imagination and Memory* (Minneapolis: Fortress Press, 1985), 14.

> "These various portrayals of David do not live in a vacuum, but are a proposed reading of reality from a certain angle of vision. Nor do these various portraits easily cohere. But when taken together, they function in a mutually corrective way, so that all these portrayals are needed to present the full reading of David made in the tradition. Any one of us as listeners to this memory may prefer one offer of truth to another. But we must try to hear them all if we would hear the full voice of memory."
>
> —Walter Brueggemann, *David's Truth* (1985), 18

It seems to me that these expressions are "history" too—the history of cultural memory. I'm not saying they are historically verifiable (although we could never disprove them either). What I am saying is, these literary portraits etch a historicizing texture on the representation of the ruler who left his mark deeply on Israel's formative literature. The writing of the David traditions was itself a historical event, or series of events, that bears consideration when we ponder "what happened" in ancient Israel. These inscriptions of charisma, brutality, loyalty, and liturgical leadership "happened" no less than did the catastrophic conflagrations and monumental buildings that left traces in the material record.

HISTORY WITH JAEL AND SISERA

We may inquire into the historicity of the time of the judges, a period about which we know relatively little apart from what is represented in Scripture. Events and institutions of the premonarchical early Iron I period would have left negligible archaeological traces in any case, because it was marked by neither monumental building projects nor massive population migrations. Destruction levels in the remains of villages and towns may be all that we have to go on when we reconstruct—or fail to reconstruct—realia having to do with the lives of peasants living in loosely organized clans and defended by small tribal militias. Miller and Hayes concede that while in their view authentic folk memory is preserved in the book of Judges, that claim can neither be proved nor disproved.[21] Nevertheless, historical criticism can help us at least obliquely with understanding the story of Jael and Sisera.[22]

21. Miller and Hayes, *History of Ancient Israel and Judah*, 84; see 84–117 for their treatment of "Earliest Israel."

22. For an overview of research on Judg. 4–5 since 1990, see Tyler Mayfield, "The Accounts of Deborah (Judges 4–5) in Recent Research," *Currents in Biblical Research* 7 (2009): 306–35.

Archaeological evidence suggests that the Canaanite city of Hazor, where Jabin was seated as king, was an impressive city until its destruction in the thirteenth century BCE. The story's assertion of political alliance between the Canaanites and the Kenites (the clan of Heber, Jael's husband) is unverifiable on historical grounds, but it is not implausible given the decentralized nature of Canaanite governmental units and the obvious advantages of alliance-making among local partners. Given that, Jael's offer of succor to a Canaanite military commander would have been unsurprising politically, but her decision to kill Sisera would have amounted to a serious political betrayal of her husband's family. Collins provides a nuanced appraisal of the historical context and its relation to our text:

> Hazor, which was allegedly destroyed in Joshua 11, and was in fact destroyed at some time during the thirteenth century, still appears in Canaanite hands in Judges 4–5. The prominence of the Philistines in the book of Judges is appropriate to the period. Also the book depicts the land of Canaan in a state of transition from the city-states of the Bronze Age to the emerging national identities of Israel, Philistia, Aram, and so forth. This transition is appropriately located in the period around 1200–1000 B.C.E. Many of the stories in Judges, however, deal with local events, which would be difficult to verify in any case. The historical value of Judges, such as it is, lies more in the general picture of conditions before the rise of the monarchy than in the specific events that are narrated.[23]

Now, these insights certainly do not constitute actual interpretation of Judges 4–5. They are guides to certain dimensions of the possible historical context that is purportedly being reflected in the text (which is not the same as saying that the text of Judges 4–5 was actually composed in that time period). But such historically oriented prolegomena or background can be helpful to keep in mind as one enters into the task of interpretation of the text itself. We might note, for example, that the enemy Canaanites are drawn with details that might be a bit hyperbolic in order to dramatize the threat that Israel faced. Susan Niditch writes this:

> Canaan was never a single political entity, but was composed of various city-states. Jabin's title, "king of Canaan," however, provides legendary stature to the defeated enemy in this epic tale. . . . The description of the enemy as armed with chariots recurs in Judges and symbolizes Israel's marginal status vis-à-vis various Canaanite and Philistine opponents (see Judg 1:19; 5:28), an important theme of the

23. Collins, *Introduction to the Hebrew Bible*, 204.

> book and an indicator of worldview. The enemy has chariots, often "chariots of iron," whereas the Israelites do not.[24]

So what is "historical" here? Not exactly that Jabin was monarch over a huge, unified region, and perhaps not even that he could muster a fleet of nine hundred chariots of iron, if that is being overstated too. But the general sense that Israel felt itself to be under dire threat by a better-equipped foe may well be historically accurate for the period and certainly is "historical" in terms of the Israelites' cultural anxiety, which is so clearly betrayed in many texts about Israelites' interactions with Canaanites. Thus we may move beyond a simplistic view of history as being only about concrete and verifiable dates, numbers, shards of pottery, layers of ash, and piles of rocks. We may think about cultural memory as a valuable historical datum in its own right, even if it cannot always be mapped transparently and simply onto a chronological timeline.

The lived experience of ancient Israelites and Judeans was real. The lived experience of the biblical writers and editors was real, too. Good historical inquiry will probe, as deeply and multidimensionally as it can, into the lived experiences of these ancient peoples and the cultural artifacts, including texts, that they left behind. Naïveté about the complexity of the historical task helps no one. It does not honor those whose witnesses we are seeking to hear and understand, and it does not serve the church or other contemporary listeners well, either. So rather than resisting the historicity problem—either by insisting that everything we read in the Bible is 100 percent accurate regardless of what the archaeological record says, or by throwing up our hands and muttering that none of it could possibly be true—we must continue to wrestle. I hope that, at least most of the time, it will be a delight for you to wrestle with the conflicted and contested views of lived experience that you encounter in the Hebrew Scriptures. And as you consider the interplay of event and representation, accord and struggle, and tradition and innovation in the written testimonies of ancient Israel, I hope it will help for you to stay mindful of these points: memory is powerful; creativity and bias are intrinsic to cultural production; and the God who calls you into encounter with the Word is real.

FOR FURTHER READING

Dever, William G. *What Did the Biblical Writers Know and When Did They Know It? What Archaeology Can Tell Us about the Reality of Ancient Israel.* Grand Rapids: Wm. B. Eerdmans Pub. Co., 2001.

Grabbe, Lester L. *Ancient Israel: What Do We Know and How Do We Know It?* New York: T&T Clark, 2007.

24. Niditch, *Judges*, 64.

Hess, Richard S. *Israelite Religions: An Archaeological and Biblical Survey*. Grand Rapids: Baker Academic, 2007.

Hoffmeier, James K. *Israel in Egypt: The Evidence for the Authenticity of the Exodus Tradition*. New York: Oxford University Press, 1997.

Provan, Iain, V. Philips Long, and Tremper Longman III. *A Biblical History of Israel.* Louisville, KY: Westminster John Knox Press, 2003.

Smith, Mark S. *The Memoirs of God: History, Memory, and the Experience of the Divine in Ancient Israel*. Minneapolis: Fortress Press, 2004.

Thompson, Thomas L. *The Mythic Past: Biblical Archaeology and the Myth of Israel.* New York: Basic Books, 1999.

4

Insiders and Outsiders

Boundaries and the Theological Imagination

The group of biblical scholars had lecture funds to spend before the end of the year, so they were meeting to consider whom to invite to speak at their school. Various possibilities were discussed. One lecturer might draw a good crowd because of his work on Wisdom literature; another had done really interesting work on the Deuteronomistic History. Then a possibility was suggested that brought the conversation to a halt: what about that scholar of Pacific Islander heritage who works on postcolonial readings of Scripture? One professor was excited at the prospect of hearing this scholar speak. "We don't do that here," she thought, "so it would be excellent for our students and our faculty to be exposed to this new perspective!" Before she could say anything, a colleague spoke up. "We don't do that here," he said firmly. No further elaboration was offered, but it was clear that he meant the comment as a negative assessment on the usefulness of inviting this potential lecturer.

"We don't do that here": identical words with vastly different meanings in different contextual moments. For one colleague, "We don't do that here" was an enthusiastic acknowledgment that their school's insularity might fruitfully be challenged. Their identity as a Scripture-reading community might be helpfully expanded through hearing about the postcolonial speaker's engagement with issues of first-world imperialism and discourses of resistance. But for another colleague, "We don't do that here" served as a powerful delineation of communal identity over against things that the community (as he saw it) intentionally declined to embrace. Certain hermeneutical boundaries were in place for good reason and ought not to be breached.

Communities and individual believers come to understand who they are when they encounter the Word of God. The encounter with Scripture yields not a one-time formation of identity but a fluid and ongoing process in which ideas of self, other, community, and God are created and re-created as particular stories, poems, motifs, and verses of Scripture transform the spiritual imagination. For believers and believing communities who look to engage Scripture as a way of knowing God and themselves, identity formation is continually enacted in a variety of complex ways through our readings of Scripture. Our understandings of personal agency and communal boundaries, too, can be profoundly shaped through encounters with Scripture. Thus particular texts and particular biblical interpretive methods have real consequences for readers and reading communities.

Texts matter. And reading strategies matter.

Consider this example. Should we read biblical texts that openly promote violence, such as holy-war texts in Deuteronomy and Joshua, as if they were inviting us personally to become violent or exhorting our faith communities to launch genocidal attacks on other communities? Surely not. Most readers and reading communities throughout the centuries have developed critical means of assessing the ways in which Scripture should and should not form us. Now, I'm sorry to say that there are those who would assent to the ancient Israelites' extermination of Canaanites and do not find that holy-war program ethically troubling. But even those folks, for the most part, would stop short of assuming that exhortations in Joshua should be applied willy-nilly to today's situations.

"Violence is not the only model of behavior on offer in the Bible, but it is not an incidental or peripheral feature, and it cannot be glossed over. The Bible witnesses not only to the innocent victim and to the God of victims but also the hungry God who devours victims and to the zeal of his human agents. And therein precisely lies its power. There is much in the Bible that is not 'worthy' of the God of the philosophers. There is also much that is not worthy of humanity, certainly much that is not worthy to serve as a model for imitation. . . . The power of the Bible is largely that it gives an unvarnished picture of human nature and of the dynamics of history, and also of religion and the things that people do in its name. . . . The biblical portrayal of human reality becomes pernicious only when it is vested with authority and assumed to reflect, without qualification or differentiation, the wisdom of God or the will of God. The Bible does not demystify or demythologize itself. But neither does it claim that the stories it tells are paradigms for human action in all times and places."

—John J. Collins, *Does the Bible Justify Violence?* (2004), 30–32

Here's another example. Some ancient Israelite texts in our Bible celebrate tricksterism. Of the several trickster figures in the Bible, probably the best known is Jacob. He plans and schemes, finagles his way into his brother's inheritance, then dodges accountability and works through dubious means to achieve economic security and freedom from reprisals. In keeping with trickster traditions across many cultures, he is subtly commended in the biblical narratives for being wily, shrewd, and skillfully deceptive. Is Jacob being presented as a moral example for us to follow? Probably not. While we can never fully know an author's motivation for portraying a character or situation in a particular way, it would seem likely that moral integrity is not the basis on which Jacob's character has been drawn for us. Nor is immorality the point. The story likely has entirely different goals motivating it, probably including an affirmation of the ability of Israelite ancestors to get the best of their enemies and a celebration of the resilience and creativity of ancestors who found themselves in difficult situations.

So is the contemporary reader right to be troubled by the Bible's valorization of manipulative and deceitful behavior in the case of Jacob? That depends on one's own ethics and the norms of the community in which one lives and ministers. According to my personal ethics and the social norms of my theological school, my church, and my family, it is indeed worthwhile to resist the Bible's lauding of tricksterism: scheming and shady dealings with another person are not generally commended in the circles in which I move. If one is looking to every biblical character as a model for contemporary behavior, then yes, I think one should be troubled by Jacob. But your own interpretive posture and temperament might be different from mine. If you are a member of a group that tends to cheer the foiling of others, Jacob might be a favorite hero of yours. Or if your ecclesial tradition does not encourage you to wrestle with Scripture at all, then you might have to look for the ways in which your tradition reframes issues so as to avoid the potential ethical conflict: in this case, perhaps your church chooses to focus on Jacob's trust in God and passes lightly over his manipulation of others.

ACKNOWLEDGING OUR SITUATEDNESS

We are continually formed by our encounters with Scripture. Every day when you pick up your Bible and turn to Deuteronomy or Luke, you enter into a richly intertextual and multifaceted conversation with current cultural and ecclesial norms, prior readings of the biblical text, and the influences (moral, spiritual, cultural) of many other texts and sources of wisdom that you honor in your life. An important part of being responsible readers is to become aware of and acknowledge the priorities and norms that shape the interpretive decisions we make. This is a chief insight of what are sometimes called "situated" readings of Scripture: readings proposed by interpreters who are alert to (at least some of) their biases and convictions and who choose, as a matter of ethics and good hermeneutics, to identify those biases and convictions as a part of the interpretive process. Like any cultural act, reading is an act of power. To acknowledge what is motivating our readings serves the interests of transparency.

It also can enrich your reading of the Bible in marvelous ways. Here's an analogy. Have you ever served in a Clinical Pastoral Education placement in a hospital? C.P.E. is a kind of apprenticeship for pastoral ministry that many seminarians undergo. It is an extraordinary integrative learning experience, because you have direct pastoral contact with patients and families, but you also read about emotional and spiritual issues associated with illness and dying, you are taught important specialized information by hands-on hospital practitioners, and you process your clinical work in a group of peers with a supervisor. At first, if you are inexperienced at offering pastoral care to the sick, the dying, the bereaved, and the anxious, you walk into each hospital room "cold," without much information and with only rudimentary skills. You know you are supposed to read the room, but you don't know much about how to do that. You try to figure out as best you can what the patient needs (which may be quite different from what the patient is talking about or asking for). You try to discern how to provide loving care and how to "get out of the way" so that the Holy Spirit can work through the encounter among all who are present. But there is a deeper level of learning that can unfold only over time in the peer-group processing and extended personal reflection. That deeper level has to do with the motivations and hopes and anxieties that you bring to each encounter with a sick or dying person. You have to learn to read yourself before you can become wise about caring for other people. Until you learn to exegete the texts of your own psyche, your family history, and your life, you will inevitably project your issues onto others and commodify them in order to meet *your* needs. That's what we do, for example, when we stay adamantly cheery and solution focused when someone is in wrenching physical pain or emotional disturbance. We are trying to make them solve *our* need—which is to not have to witness their pain—rather than being truly present to them in their anguish.[1]

Just so, when we read Scripture, we inevitably bring into that reading experience who we are, what we care about, and what we are trying to avoid

1. Among the many fine resources on pastoral care in a clinical setting is Pamela Cooper-White's *Shared Wisdom: Use of the Self in Pastoral Care and Counseling* (Minneapolis: Fortress Press, 2004).

or suppress. Until we become wise about reading ourselves—which includes reading our communities and our history—we will be at the mercy of our subjugated desire, our unwitting narcissism, our cultural ignorance or arrogance, and our anxiety about being vulnerable in openness to the text and the Holy Spirit. Hence it is a salutary thing to be alert to one's own biases, goals, and concerns when one is engaging in biblical interpretation. It's also politically important, since every act of interpretation is an act of power. This is a chief insight of "situated" readings. When we are aware of the commitments and limitations of our communities and our social location, we can engage our whole selves in the act of interpretation in a way that can be illuminating rather than misdirected, abusive, or overcompensatory.

Among the many kinds of situated or contextual interpretations these days are feminist and womanist readings, queer readings, and postcolonial readings. We will explore issues involved in these kinds of readings below. But first, two preliminary notes are in order.

LIBERATION AND POLITICS

Liberation theology has rightly been seen as the original seedbed for the development of situated readings of many different kinds. Liberation theology has had an impact on biblical interpretation since the 1970s, when it emerged in South and Central America, North America, and Africa. What is liberation theology? Simply put, it is a practice of reading Scripture and doing theology from a starting place of advocacy for the poor and the oppressed. Liberation theologians such as James Cone, Gustavo Gutiérrez, and Rosemary Radford Ruether have argued that many biblical traditions witness to a "preferential option for the poor." That is, the Bible shows God consistently and passionately uplifting the poor and fighting on behalf of the oppressed against their oppressors. Central to much liberation-theological exegesis are the twin themes of the exodus and prophetic witness against social injustice. Arguing that abstract eschatologized theologies of salvation are inadequate as resources for real people in oppressive contexts, liberation theologians insist that God's deliverance is meant to be experienced fully and concretely in real situations of suffering. Particular focuses in liberation theology have been Latino/a liberation, African and African American liberation, and feminism. Located somewhat more uncomfortably within liberation theology is advocacy for the liberation of gay, lesbian, and transgendered people from the oppression of homophobia, heteronormativity, and rigid binary views of gender. The discomfort of some liberation theologians on these issues may be traced, at least in part, to the fact that some ecclesial communities, such as the black church, that have traditionally supported liberation-theological readings tend to endorse androcentric, heteronormative views of human sexuality.

My second preliminary observation is a cautionary note about the politics of this discussion in the biblical studies academy. Many influential biblical scholars writing today seem to have little self-consciousness about dismissing any interpretive approach in which the author identifies her own social location, commitments, and goals of reading rather than trumpeting her methodological position as if it were a universally true and "natural" way of engaging the text. John Barton's book *The Nature of Biblical Criticism* (2007) proposes ten theses about the importance of seeking what he calls the "plain sense" of the biblical text. In his thesis #6, he makes the claim: "Attempts to collapse the reading of texts into a single process, as in some proposals to undertake a (postcritical) 'theological reading' of the text and in certain 'committed' or 'advocacy' approaches, are misconceived."[2]

It is a fundamental insight of much recent scholarship that in fact *all* readings are committed to ideological goals; it's just that not all interpreters are self-aware about their own biases or candid with their audiences about them. Barton presents as neutral and universal his views on the Bible and methods, without any concern to reflect on his situatedness as a white male European scholar in a financially vested position at a powerful Western university (Oxford). Yet the topics he selects for discussion, the ways in which he frames the relevant issues and presents his arguments, and the questions that he does not engage are all conditioned by his cultural norms and "situatedness" as an interpreter. Barton's dismissiveness toward situated readings is still the dominant attitude in Western academic biblical scholarship, in my view.[3] Self-consciously contextual readings are marked by many scholars in North America and Western Europe as special, nonnormative readings that are of a different and lesser kind than so-called neutral and objective scholarship. All I can do in these pages is to invite you to consider such claims to neutrality from a perspective of healthy skepticism.

Since biblical interpretation has a significant and lasting impact on identity formation for many believing readers, we would do well to look at how Israel, the believer, and the outsider are constructed in Scripture as speakers or as those who are silenced, as acting subjects or as objectified nonsubjects, as vested members of community or as those kept outside of community. This question

2. John Barton, *The Nature of Biblical Criticism* (Louisville, KY: Westminster John Knox Press, 2007), 6.

3. This is to take nothing away from the North American theological schools famous for their commitment to social justice and liberation theology. In those ranks, I number Episcopal Divinity School in Cambridge, Massachusetts; Union Theological Seminary in New York City; Drew Theological School in Madison, New Jersey; and Iliff School of Theology in Denver, Colorado.

of the social construction of insiders and outsiders matters deeply because so many contemporary believers look to Scripture for signals about how to be faithful, how to love God, and how to define our own communities of faith.

TROUBLING SCRIPTURE TEXTS

Here's the bad news, and there is no way to sugarcoat it: the Hebrew Scriptures contain rhetorics and stories that harm, distort, and silence. Whatever their views of the holiness and authority of biblical texts, folks from many different ecclesial traditions have come to acknowledge that some dimensions of scriptural signifying have been harmful for certain readers (especially, but not only, women and queer believers) and troubling for the church. How? Let me count the ways. Women characters in Scripture are few and far between, and the females who are featured in narratives are male-identified; that is, they are narratologically described and defined by their relationships as wives of men, sexual partners of men, daughters of men, or mothers of sons. The implied audience of huge swaths of the Hebrew Scriptures (including numerous texts in the legal material, the Psalms, the prophetic corpus, and Wisdom literature) is rhetorically constructed as male, something we can see by gendered constraints to the topics discussed and, sometimes, by the grammatically masculine gender in Hebrew pronouns and verbs of direct address (the masculine "you"). The prophetic corpus regularly employs images of battering and sexual violence against women as metaphors for how God will treat Israel or Israel's enemies, along with tropes gendered as feminine that imply cultural shaming and emasculation for the male audience. These tropes, such as the likening of terrified warriors to women writhing in labor, serve both to underline the androcentric focus of the texts and to render femaleness itself as shameful.

More troubling texts? Race and ethnicity are usually construed in the Hebrew Scriptures as negative markers of Otherness over against a monolithically conceived Israelite identity. When an outsider is accepted into the community, it is at the cost of the erasure of the person's prior ethnic identity (as we see with Hagar the Egyptian, Rahab of Jericho, and Ruth the Moabite). Hostile militarism directed against ethnic Others, xenophobia, and even imperatives to Israel to commit genocide based on targets' ethnicity and geographical location—these can be found in the Pentateuch, the prophetic oracles against the nations, and elsewhere. Some texts (such as the commandment to circumcise all in a household including one's slaves: Gen. 17:12–13) assume the holding of slaves, without even the faintest sign of awareness about an ethical problem with slaveholding. No generative same-sex romantic relationships are described in the entire corpus of the Hebrew Scriptures—at least not openly, although some scholars have raised the question of whether sexual or romantic intimacy may be being signaled by subtle cues in the narratives about David's relationship with Jonathan or the story of Ruth clinging to Naomi. Laws in the Torah forbid sexual contact between men, naming homosexual intimacy as an abomination for which those involved deserve to be cut off from their people. Numerous texts in the Hebrew Scriptures authorize an imperialistic attitude on the part of Israel toward other nations. Even in Isaiah, that most theologically inclusive of prophetic books, the nations are portrayed as crawling to Zion, cowed and licking dust (45:14; 49:23).

I do not intend to reduce the powerful witness of the Hebrew Scriptures to these problematic dimensions of difficult texts. There are extraordinary, life-giving, transformative texts and images within the Old Testament. I have dedicated my life to seeking wisdom, truth, and holiness in its pages. But my position is that the misogyny, androcentrism, ethnocentrism, homophobia, and imperialism that we find in the Bible are distorted human perspectives not willed by God and disastrously harmful to human flourishing. If you happen to disagree on one or another of those points—if "feminist" is a pejorative term in your ecclesial tradition, or if you see homosexuality as counter to the will of God—I encourage you to keep reading simply to understand better what is at stake for many readers in these debates. You will assuredly have your own troubling texts, even if they are different from mine, and I hope that these discussions will equip you to wrestle faithfully with your own challenges.

In what follows, we will explore key issues that are debated in biblical studies concerning representations of gender, sexuality, and imperialist rhetoric. Because the resources that exist to further conversation on these issues may not be as well known as resources addressing traditional hermeneutical methods, the Documentary Hypothesis, and the history of ancient Israel, I will spend some time describing the kinds of guides that are available.

FEMINIST AND WOMANIST READINGS

Feminist biblical hermeneutics privileges women's experience as a source of knowing and declines the claims (implicit and overt) of patriarchy that male bodies and males' experiences should be normative and authoritative for the lives of all human beings. Womanist readings share many goals of feminist interpretation but proceed from a grounding specifically in the experience and lived wisdom of black women. Women readers have long had difficulties with the Hebrew Scriptures' presentations of women and women's agency in the lives of ancient Israelite and Judean communities. It may be true that male readers also have been disturbed by gendered rhetoric generally and portrayal of women's bodies and agency in the Bible. After all, these things are presumably matters of concern to all readers of Scripture who care about human flourishing, not just those readers who self-identify as female. But as of this writing, the number of male biblical commentators who have said anything sustained on the subject of gender construction is still relatively small.

Understanding how to honor their own experience and see themselves as agents rather than mere objects of males' actions and perceptions has been and continues to be a tremendous challenge for women in patriarchal cultures across the globe. When one's sacred texts reinforce the idea that the male is normative and that the female is Other and dangerous—as the Hebrew Scriptures do in many and varied ways—women learn implicitly to position themselves on the margins of their faith community and on the margins of the traditions of Scripture; and men learn to position women on the margins as well. While female-gender issues have been obliquely engaged from reactionary and harmful perspectives throughout the history of male-dominated religious cultures (male-gendered identity being taken as normative and therefore assumed rather than critiqued), gender has only recently been considered an appropriate subject for explicit critical investigation in biblical studies. (The critical attention within biblical scholarship paid to the subfield of masculinity studies is still minuscule: only a very few biblical scholars are doing this work.) Some voices are missing entirely from this discussion. Some feminists have rejected the Bible outright as a source of useful insight for women and no longer consider Scripture to be authoritative in any way. They feel that the risks of facing the misogynist perspectives in many Scripture texts so outweigh the possible benefits of encountering its more fruitful texts that they have chosen to stay away from engagement with Scripture as an authority for their spiritual journeys.

In Hebrew Bible studies, feminist and womanist attention to gender has generally pursued three related but distinct impulses. In older feminist scholarship, we saw heavy emphasis on the recovery of women's stories and women's moral agency within Scripture as significant both for ancient Israel and for the contemporary reader. This interpretive impulse has remained lively to the present day, with women's groups and feminist biblical exegetes continuing to attend to the handful of women who are given any depth of characterization at all in the Hebrew Scriptures. Groundbreaking early examples of this kind of work are Phyllis Trible's *God and the Rhetoric of Sexuality* (1978) and *Texts of Terror: Literary-Feminist Readings of Biblical Narratives* (1984). In the latter work, Trible performs literary-critical readings of the stories of four biblical women: Hagar, Tamar (the one raped by David's son Amnon), the Levite's concubine from Judges, and Jephthah's daughter. Attending closely to language and imagery, Trible eloquently portrays the abjection, pathos, and injustice of each biblical woman's situation. In a stroke of artistic genius, Trible heads each chapter with the poignant image of a tombstone inscribed with the name of the woman and a verse that evokes either the Suffering Servant of Isaiah or the sufferings of Christ:

- HAGAR, Egyptian Slave Woman: She was wounded for our transgressions; she was bruised for our iniquities.
- TAMAR, Princess of Judah: A woman of sorrows and acquainted with grief.
- AN UNNAMED WOMAN, Concubine from Bethlehem: Her body was broken and given to many.
- THE DAUGHTER OF JEPHTHAH, Virgin in Gilead: My God, my God, why hast thou forsaken her?

In what has justly become a famous passage, Trible writes of Hagar:

> Hagar foreshadows Israel's pilgrimage of faith through contrast. As a maid in bondage, she flees from suffering. Yet she experiences exodus without liberation, revelation without salvation, wilderness without covenant, wanderings without land, promise without fulfillment, and unmerited exile without return. This Egyptian slave woman is stricken, smitten by God, and afflicted for the transgressions of Israel. She is bruised for the iniquities of Sarah and Abraham; upon her is the chastisement that makes them whole.[4]

Another work in the vein of recovering ancient women's experience is womanist interpreter Wilda C. Gafney's *Daughters of Miriam: Women Prophets in Ancient Israel* (2008). Studies of prophecy before this work had focused almost entirely on male intermediaries. Gafney demonstrates that one can do much more with the topic of female prophets than nod in passing to Miriam, Deborah, and Huldah. She examines the evidence for female intermediaries in the ancient Near East, focusing on original texts from Mari, Nineveh, and Emar. She carefully explores the representations of female prophets in the Hebrew Scriptures, including not only Miriam, Deborah, and Huldah but also No'adiah (Neh. 6:14), an anonymous female prophet in the book of Isaiah (8:3), the "daughters" who will prophesy in Joel and are said to prophesy in Ezekiel, and the daughters of Heman (1 Chron. 25:5–8). She considers evidence for mixed-gender and all-female prophetic and liturgical guilds in ancient Israel, assesses reflections on female prophets in rabbinic and Christian tradition, and engages in constructive work to identify other female prophets

4. Phyllis Trible, *Texts of Terror: Literary-Feminist Readings of Biblical Narratives* (Minneapolis: Fortress Press, 1984), 28.

in the Bible even when they were not named explicitly as such. Considering the roles of women in prophetic, musical, and scribal guilds, Gafney offers this:

> The term *patriarchy* is an inadequate description of Israelite society. . . . The whole notion of "top-down hierarchy" as a framework for understanding Israelite society is undercut by the organizations of these guilds and their internal hierarchies. The authority and influence of these women extend beyond the circle of their guilds. The public and performative aspect of the work of each type of guild means that these women exert influence on a wider, mixed-gender, public sphere. This influence is not mediated through male authority.[5]

Two other illustrative works in the area of recovering biblical women's voices and stories are Athalya Brenner's *I Am . . . : Biblical Women Tell Their Own Stories* (2005) and Jacqueline E. Lapsley's *Whispering the Word: Hearing Women's Stories in the Old Testament* (2005). The flood of works in this stream of scholarship, which ranges from comparative cross-cultural work to exegetical soundings to creative reconstructions, shows no signs of abating. Many of these works are highly accessible to the church.[6]

A second impulse within feminist biblical scholarship has been to research and reclaim the divine feminine (to the extent that is possible) and the paradigmatic feminine in motifs and metaphors within the Hebrew Bible, notably in the personified figure of Wisdom (e.g., in Prov. 8) and in the personified figure of Zion as the city of Jerusalem. Exemplary here is the work of Christl M. Maier. In her *Daughter Zion, Mother Zion: Gender, Space, and the Sacred in Ancient Israel* (2008), Maier explores social constructions of sacred space gendered as female in the ancient Near East and analyzes the biblical metaphorization of Jerusalem and the people of Israel as daughter, whore, wounded female body, and mother. Insights abound in her work; it is a valuable resource for all who want to think about gendered constructions of body, voice, and community in the Hebrew Scriptures. Maier explains:

> The female personification of the city acknowledges that humans have bodies and build place relations through their bodies. Since the varying portraits of the female city construe Jerusalem's history, they form a multivoiced discourse that envisions the relations between city, population, and the deity from different angles, yet

5. Wilda C. Gafney, *Daughters of Miriam: Women Prophets in Ancient Israel* (Minneapolis: Fortress Press, 2008), 130, with original emphasis.

6. An accessible introductory treatment is Linda Day and Carolyn Pressler, eds., *Engaging the Bible in a Gendered World: An Introduction to Feminist Biblical Interpretation in Honor of Katharine Doob Sakenfeld* (Louisville, KY: Westminster John Knox Press, 2006). Another important resource is the series called A Feminist Companion to the Bible, 2nd ser., edited by Athalya Brenner. The volume on Judges was published by Sheffield Academic Press in 1999.

> corresponds with social relations between human bodies. In their variety, these perspectives may invite modern readers to reflect upon their definition of sacred spaces and to think about the relationship between gender, topography, ideology, and experience in the social spaces they produce.[7]

This conceptual work can be helpful for Christian feminists thinking about the gendered space of the church and other constructed spaces as well.

A third impulse in feminist and womanist biblical scholarship is characterized by active and creative subversion of patriarchal (mis)understandings and (mal)formations of women's spirits, voices, bodies, agency, and power, both in Scripture texts and in the reception of those texts in androcentric interpretive communities. While all feminist works engage in this critical subversion to some degree, I highlight here works that are centrally focused on the prophetic work of challenge and deconstruction. Women scholars, and occasionally a male scholar such as Robert P. Carroll, have critiqued the language of sexual violence in the prophets, paying special attention to the power of metaphor to organize and direct a community's conceptualization of itself, its history, God, and the ongoing covenant relationship. The work of womanist scholar Renita J. Weems, *Battered Love: Marriage, Sex, and Violence in the Hebrew Prophets* (1995), is often cited in this regard. There have been a number of studies of biblical rhetorics of sex and gender since the publication of that book, including Yvonne Sherwood's *The Prostitute and the Prophet: Hosea's Marriage in Literary-Theoretical Perspective* (1996), Alice A. Keefe's *Woman's Body and the Social Body in Hosea* (2001), Gale A. Yee's *Poor Banished Children of Eve: Woman as Evil in the Hebrew Bible* (2003), and Hilary B. Lipka's *Sexual Transgression in the Hebrew Bible* (2006), all of which examine the role of constructions of sexuality in the establishment and maintenance of social boundaries in ancient Israel or in the reception history of relevant biblical texts.

Womanist readings of the Bible take as a starting point the experiences of African, African American, and other black women. It is still a nascent field within biblical studies proper; considerably more work has been done in womanist theology and womanist ethics than in womanist biblical scholarship as such. One womanist scholar could note as a sign of the growth of the field that, as of 2005, "more than one hundred women of African ancestry" attend the annual meetings of the American Academy of Religion or the Society of Biblical Literature each year.[8] The statistic is indeed heartening for those of us who support womanist inquiry. But it must be acknowledged that the number

7. Christl M. Maier, *Daughter Zion, Mother Zion: Gender, Space, and the Sacred in Ancient Israel* (Minneapolis: Fortress Press, 2008), 217.

8. Katie G. Cannon, Alison P. Gise Johnson, and Angela D. Sims, "Womanist Works in Word," *Journal of Feminist Studies in Religion* 21 (2005): 135.

represents a tiny fraction of the total membership of those organizations, which have many thousands of members each, and most womanists do not specialize in biblical studies.

Womanist biblical criticism lifts up a crucially important nexus of questions having to do with gender and race or ethnicity. As Gafney describes it,

> Womanist biblical scholarship pays close attention to the language and grammar of hierarchies and relationships in the text, its context, and its community of readers. Although womanists are concerned first with their implications for women of color, their children and/or partners, our work finally champions all people, spoken to, spoken of, and ignored by the text. While black male sexism and white female racism and classism delineate an obvious perimeter of womanist discourse, women of color have reflected on their whole identities in relation to men and other women, children and adults, within and across cultural, social, and economic lines, for as long as those distinctions have been applied.[9]

Feminist and womanist biblical interpreters do not limit their purview to examining sacred texts and reception history only. They also seek to inquire critically into white privilege and to destabilize the androcentric, Eurocentric, and heteronormative nature of biblical scholarship within Western academic culture as a set of intellectual practices and unspoken norms. For many of its practitioners, feminist hermeneutics invites a subversive reframing of the fundamental epistemological and hermeneutical priorities of the white- and male-dominated Western academy.

> "Feminist epistemology is not only a critique of ideology, that is, a questioning of the cultural inscriptions of gender hierarchies—it is as well a critique of conventional norms and procedures in any given discipline and field of study. In this sense it is a critique of phallogocentrism, the interlocking regimes of truth that have imposed themselves on various fields of study. By defining the authoritative posture of the literary approach to the Bible as "the objective phallacy," I sought to establish one of the basic insights of feminist epistemology, namely that all knowledge is political, including and especially male-centered knowledge about canonic texts like the Bible."
>
> —Esther Fuchs, "Biblical Feminisms: Knowledge, Theory and Politics in the Study of Women in the Hebrew Bible" (2008), 209

9. Wilda C. Gafney, "A Black Feminist Approach to Biblical Studies," *Encounter* 67 (2006): 392.

Feminist interpretation is itself a contested site of struggle these days as practitioners try to negotiate tensions among varieties of models for feminist theory and praxis. One highly visible conflict has been generated between those on the one hand who see feminism as dedicated to empowering women and the feminine as those have been traditionally understood, and those who are influenced by postmodern gender studies and thus see gender and sexual identity as performed along a socially constructed spectrum. The latter group stands with pansexual, transgendered, and intersex persons in opposition to understandings of human embodiment based on normative sex-and-gender binaries (male/female, straight/gay). Some of them are impatient with what they construe as the misguided identity politics and biological essentialism of those who remain committed to working on behalf of women and girls. Conversely, some traditional or "second-wave" feminists have critiqued postmodern feminists and gender warriors for failing fully and unequivocally to engage the advocacy goals that they see as intrinsic to feminism. The scholarly debate around women's studies, gender theory, and feminist praxis is lively indeed. For biblical interpreters who want to engage the issues, there are many avenues into this fascinating set of cultural and ethical discourses.[10]

AFRICAN AND AFRICAN AMERICAN BIBLICAL HERMENEUTICS

The field of African American biblical scholarship shares with feminist and womanist analysis a high estimation of the need for cultural critique. Relatively few book-length resources as yet exist specifically in the area of African American academic scholarship on the Hebrew Scriptures. But there is a rich trove of works treating the Bible in African American spirituality, literature, art, and music. One important resource is a collection edited by Vincent L. Wimbush titled *African Americans and the Bible: Sacred Texts and Social Textures* (2003), which offers sixty-three contributions from theological scholars and professors of such disciplines as English, history, and sociology. The essays analyze the roles and functions of Scripture in many diverse arenas within the reception history of the Bible, including slave narratives, African American poetry, constructions of the political role of the black church, Caribbean Rastafarianism, and African American folk healing. A resource more focused on

10. An excellent resource on current debates in women's studies is Robyn Wiegman, ed., *Women's Studies on Its Own: A Next Wave Reader in Institutional Change* (Durham, NC: Duke University Press, 2002).

academic interpretation is Michael Joseph Brown's *Blackening of the Bible: The Aims of African American Biblical Scholarship* (2004), which provides detailed analyses of the hermeneutics of many African American biblical scholars working today. Brown problematizes the Eurocentrism of historical-critical methodologies and suggests areas in which African American biblical scholarship can be strengthened as it continues to develop.

To their analysis of biblical reception history, practitioners of African biblical hermeneutics add a heightened dimension of critique of the legacy of Western colonialism. In feminist, womanist, African American, and African biblical hermeneutics alike, we see a deep attentiveness to the embodied experiences and real-world challenges of believers struggling to live faithfully in and through encounters with Scripture. Listen to the passionate way in which African biblicist Nyambura J. Njoroge describes what is at stake:

> Do we speak of a Christianity that appears impotent before bushfires of poverty, violence, ignorance, disease, corruption, and greed that are sweeping the continent [of Africa]? What does this Bible, which in my Gikuyu language is called *Ibuku ria Ngai*, "the Book of God," have to offer in the midst of bloodshed among the youth of Africa, of the prime ages of fifteen to forty? What can a book offer that is used to exploit its illiterate and ignorant listeners, the elderly women and men, who watch helplessly when their children and grandchildren die, leaving no name behind to carry on life? . . . What can a book offer that is used by the so-called messengers of the good news to stigmatize and ostracize those dying from HIV/AIDS? What can a book offer that has been used to keep Africans, women, and slaves "in their place"? . . . Is this book a curse or a blessing to the weary and lamenting people of Africa? . . . My fellow Africans, enough is enough! We have lived with too many lies. We must get up, arise (*talitha cum*), and discover the truth for ourselves. We call on our technicians, our biblical scholars, to come to our aid—to help us read, hear, perceive, interpret, and liberate the word of life promised in the Bible, in the face of the bushfires spreading throughout Africa. We call on our sisters and brothers to help us unveil layers of distorted messages; these messages have been added to a message already hidden in layers of historical, cultural, social, economic, and religious realities that shaped the writing of the Bible over one thousand years, let alone its translation into many languages. . . . For African Christianity to be life-giving, creative, healing, and authentic, African biblical scholars, albeit a small number, must rescue the Bible from the misuse and misinterpretation that has disadvantaged faithful followers of Christ, especially women.[11]

11. Nyambura J. Njoroge, "The Bible and African Christianity: A Curse or a Blessing?" in *Other Ways of Reading: African Women and the Bible*, ed. Musa W. Dube (Atlanta: Society of Biblical Literature; Geneva: WCC Publications, 2001), 213–14.

Here Njoroge positions African hermeneutics as a kind of prophetic witness that is urgently needed not just by believers in Africa but by all those who follow Jesus Christ.

QUEER READINGS

Recent years have seen the flourishing of queer interpretation of Scripture, which is a new and still emerging subfield within biblical studies. Queer hermeneutics developed out of more general work on cultural constructions of sexuality and power done by theorists such as French philosopher and sociologist Michel Foucault and American gender theorist Judith Butler.[12] Queer biblical readings seek to unmask and destabilize heteronormativity, which, simply defined, is the assumption that heterosexual identity, relationships, and behaviors should be normative for all persons. Queer readings seek to recover and affirm the stories, voices, and interpretive practices of lesbian, gay, bisexual, transgendered, and gender-queer persons, as well as to challenge homophobia and other kinds of prejudice against sexual minorities wherever those may be seen within biblical texts and within the history of interpretation of Scripture.

Two important collections of essays in this field are *Take Back the Word: A Queer Reading of the Bible* (edited by Robert E. Goss and Mona West; 2000) and *Queer Commentary and the Hebrew Bible* (edited by Ken Stone; 2001). Here are three representative insights from the panoply of queer readings to be found in these resources:

> God's words "Let my people go!" is a command to come out of physical bondage to not only reclaim our bodies but also to rebuild a broken black humanity that includes lesbians, gays, bisexuals, and transgender people. (Irene Monroe)[13]
>
> Although I was never an active participant in second-wave feminism's policing of lesbians, I have read enough of that history to feel, breathing down my neck, their criticism for having shared the male gaze. It seems, then, that . . . achieving solidarity with feminist colleagues must come at the expense of the distinctiveness of my lesbian erotic

12. Web sites dedicated to the work of Michel Foucault include http://www.michel-foucault.com/ and http://www.csun.edu/~hfspc002/foucault.home.html and http://foucault.info/. A Web site for the work of Judith Butler is http://www.theory.org.uk/ctr-butl.htm. A good general introduction to queer studies is Nikki Sullivan's *A Critical Introduction to Queer Theory* (New York: New York University Press, 2003).

13. Irene Monroe, "When and Where I Enter, Then the Whole Race Enters with Me: Que(e)rying Exodus," in *Take Back the Word: A Queer Reading of the Bible*, ed. Robert E. Goss and Mona West (Cleveland: Pilgrim Press, 2000), 85.

desire for, and appreciation of, other women. But it does not have to be this way. A lesbian gaze is not a male gaze and it does not objectify Bathsheba all over again. In fact, maybe it can, instead, spring her free from her entrapment to the male gaze. (Deryn Guest)[14]

YHWH's culturally ascribed manhood . . . may paradoxically be *surrendered* from the start by virtue of Hosea's informed decision to marry a woman whose (supposed) "promiscuous" or "whoring" character is already known. . . . The book does expose the inability of masculinities—including divine masculinities—ever to establish themselves over against the "feminine term" in a consistent and nonproblematic fashion. And precisely this recognition, that even so relentlessly patriarchal a text as Hosea is in the end not entirely successful in constructing a consistent and secure representation of manhood, may allow us to imagine a space for alternative, even queer, scenarios that could involve the surrender, rather than the embrace, of the structures of agonistic masculinity. (Ken Stone)[15]

Also worthy of mention is the one-volume *Queer Bible Commentary* (2006), which focuses exegetically on biblical texts of particular interest to gay and lesbian readers of Scripture and their allies.

"A queer reading goes beyond and even challenges homosexual liberationist readings, which argue for gay and lesbian inclusion from the premise of the naturalness of homosexuality and against claims that sex and sexual desire between men or between women is neither natural nor good. *Gay resistance* challenges Christianity on two levels, that of justice and in relation to the 'essence' of God and creation. *Queer theory*, on the other hand, challenges the essentialist notions of the former since it considers sexual identity as a cultural fabrication, and allows for a broader scope of sex and gender possibilities than the homosexual and heterosexual binary."

—Jeremy Punt, "Queer Theory Intersecting with Postcolonial Theory in Biblical Interpretation" (2006), 32, with original emphasis

Work important for queer biblical studies includes anthropological and sociological analyses of understandings of the body and performances of gender in the culture of ancient Israel. Here one might consult feminist studies

14. Deryn Guest, "Looking Lesbian at the Bathing Bathsheba," *Biblical Interpretation* 16 (2008): 238–39.

15. Ken Stone, "Lovers and Raisin Cakes: Food, Sex, and Divine Insecurity in Hosea," in *Queer Commentary and the Hebrew Bible*, ed. Ken Stone (Cleveland: Pilgrim Press, 2001), 138–39, with original emphasis.

more generally and also works such as Ken Stone's *Sex, Honor and Power in the Deuteronomistic History* (1996) and Jon L. Berquist's *Controlling Corporeality: The Body and the Household in Ancient Israel* (2002).

POSTCOLONIAL CRITICISM

For the past five decades, scholars have shown a passionate interest in examining, critiquing, and resisting the discourses of empire. Postcolonial criticism has supplied biblical studies with a compelling and supple vocabulary for theorizing power relations in imperialistic cultural and textual practices from ancient times to the present day. Here biblical scholars have tended to draw especially on the work of Gayatri Spivak and Homi Bhabha.[16] The norms and unexpressed assumptions of Eurocentric biblical scholarship have come in for critique as part of the postcolonial endeavor. A leader in this work has been Fernando F. Segovia, whose book *Decolonizing Biblical Studies* (2000) provides a vigorous articulation of postcolonial objections to the historical-critical hermeneutics and pedagogies that are favored in Western theological schools.[17] Postcolonial critics have worked to destabilize the ways in which Western intellectual elites have—wittingly or unwittingly—controlled conversations about biblical history, hermeneutics, and the supposed credentials of interpreters. Some of this work is going on in North American theological schools. Other vibrant dimensions of the conversation are unfolding in venues across the globe and across a wide variety of social contexts, including in indigenous Bible-reading communities in the developing world.

Postcolonial criticism has transparent and important applications to Old Testament studies for several reasons. First, the Hebrew Scriptures were produced by the scribal elites of two nations—Israel and Judah—whose national experiences were continuously defined by either the threat of military subjugation or the reality of colonization by Assyria, Babylon, or Persia. In turbulent and conflicted ways, many texts in the Hebrew Scriptures reflect on the pressure experienced by exilic Judah and postexilic Yehud to assimilate gracefully or to resist colonization. Theological discourses and political groups

16. The oeuvres of Gayatri Chakravorty Spivak and Homi K. Bhabha are substantial. Representative works of value for the biblical interpreter eager to learn about postcolonialism are Spivak's *A Critique of Postcolonial Reason: Toward a History of the Vanishing Present* (Cambridge, MA: Harvard University Press, 1999) and Bhabha's *The Location of Culture* (London: Routledge, 1994; repr., 2005).

17. Fernando F. Segovia, *Decolonizing Biblical Studies: A View from the Margins* (Maryknoll, NY: Orbis Books, 2000).

represented in the books of Jeremiah, Ezekiel, Ezra–Nehemiah, Esther, and Daniel are defined in part by their responses to the complicated question of whether to embrace or resist the imperial power of Babylon and Persia.

A second reason that postcolonial criticism matters for biblical studies: ancient Israel's own founding narratives are deeply implicated in colonialist rhetoric and fantasies of empire. The central trope of the exodus story creates a subjugated and powerless Israel that throws off the shackles of oppression. The traditions of the conquest aggressively authorize Israel's own subjugation and colonization of indigenous Canaanites in a utopian "promised land." The insistent fractures running through Israel's self-narration as both conquered and conqueror beg for sophisticated postcolonial analysis.

A third factor that may interest biblical readers in postcolonial criticism is the vital role that interpretations of the Bible have played in the evangelization and colonization of territories and cultures deemed "primitive" or "savage" by Westerners. This is an urgent matter for ethics and cultural studies that should be considered by every devout reader of Scripture—and especially readers credentialed as interpreters via their participation in the Western academy and in first-world churches.

Postcolonial thought ranges creatively over a vast landscape of topics. Here are a few of the issues that postcolonial theorists like to mull over a mocha latte, a salty lassi, or a glass of soursop juice:

- explorations of cultural and ethnic hybridity as a feature of postmodern identity
- ways to understand the subjectivity of the subaltern: the agency, voice, and self-understanding of an oppressed, colonized, or nondominant-culture person
- diaspora as a site of physical, cultural, or symbolic dislocation that problematizes notions of homeland, heritage, nostalgia, and belonging
- social or cultural mimicry as a survival tactic of the colonized

It is a tenet of postcolonial criticism that practices of cultural imperialism seek to erase or commodify the identities of persons and communities in service of the colonizer's own anxious, self-aggrandizing narrative of identity. And the question of identity formation is crucially important in the Hebrew Scriptures. From the story of the Garden of Eden to the call of Abraham to the Sinai traditions to the witness of the prophets, we watch as Hebrew Scripture texts grapple with issues having to do with the spiritual, ethical, and political identity of the people of God:

> You are dust, and to dust you shall return! (Gen. 3:19)

> You shall be holy, for I the Lord your God am holy! (Lev. 19:2)

> You shall love the LORD your God with all your heart, and with all your soul, and with all your might. (Deut. 6:5)

> You who fear the LORD, praise him! (Ps. 22:23)

> Do justice, love mercy, and walk humbly with your God! (cf. Mic. 6:8)

The imperative voicing of these sorts of biblical rhetoric seeks to mold Israelite identity in particular ways. But the imperative is undercut and contested by biblical texts that betray a deep uncertainty about identity in the presence of the Other or in the presence of God.

> Jacob said, "I will not let you go, unless you bless me." So he said to him, "What is your name?" And he said, "Jacob." Then the man said, "You shall no longer be called Jacob, but Israel, for you have striven with God and with humans, and have prevailed." (Gen 32:26–28)

> [The people said to Moses,] "'Is this not the very thing we told you in Egypt, 'Let us alone and let us serve the Egyptians'? For it would have been better for us to serve the Egyptians than to die in the wilderness." (Exod. 14:12)

> [The LORD said,] "Israel has sinned; they have transgressed my covenant that I imposed on them. They have taken some of the devoted things; they have stolen, they have acted deceitfully, and they have put them among their own belongings. Therefore the Israelites are unable to stand before their enemies; they turn their backs to their enemies, because they have become a thing devoted for destruction themselves." (Josh. 7:11–12)

> [Job answered,]
> "God gives me up to the ungodly,
> and casts me into the hands of the wicked.
> I was at ease, and he broke me in two;
> he seized me by the neck and dashed me to pieces."
> (Job 16:11–12)

> Vanity of vanities, says the Teacher, vanity of vanities! All is vanity. (Eccl. 1:2)

In the Hebrew Scriptures, Israel is continually in the process of formation, re-formation, and fracture. Israel's body and Israel's land are written and rewritten, over and over again. Postcolonial criticism can help us to think well about the power dynamics involved in the inscriptions and erasures of identity performed by these sacred texts as they "colonize" their implied audiences.

> "Every piece of land can be contested. Every site has a history of its own, full of 'inscriptions' left by diverse groups of people who inhabited it over a long period of time. In its effort to write a national history, colonial discourse erases the prior history of the territory and sees it as an empty space for its own history to unfold in time. The land is seen as empty, ready to accept new people and their narratives. From a postcolonial perspective, however, it is viewed as a palimpsest, written and overwritten by successive inscriptions, where there are always traces of previous inscriptions, other histories, and other memories."
>
> —Uriah Y. Kim, "Postcolonial Criticism: Who Is the Other in the Book of Judges?" (2007), 176

Feminist, womanist, queer, and postcolonial criticisms address themselves to the construction of insiders and outsiders, both in texts and in the embodied social and religious practices of communities of interpretation. As you consider how you might be called to wrestle with insider/outsider issues in Scripture and in biblical studies, two final recommendations of literature may help here. These are two collections of essays that lift up the voices of interpreters speaking from many different kinds of margins or liminal spaces in biblical studies. The first is *Voices from the Margin: Interpreting the Bible in the Third World* (1991; 3rd ed., 2006). The second is a follow-up volume, *Still at the Margins: Biblical Scholarship Fifteen Years after the Voices from the Margin* (2008). The editor of both volumes, seasoned postcolonial critic R. S. Sugirtharajah, tracks indicators of progress and lack of progress in the postcolonial push to decenter the Western academic enterprise of biblical interpretation.[18]

JAEL AND SISERA: TRANSGENDERED AND COLONIZED

Let's reread the story of Jael and Sisera once more together, this time paying attention to signifiers of gender and colonization. A number of fascinating possibilities play out along the axis of gender analysis here. A paradigm of female battle savvy and male ineffectualness is established at the beginning

18. Relevant also is another book by R. S. Sugirtharajah, *Postcolonial Criticism and Biblical Interpretation* (Oxford: Oxford University Press, 2002). See also R. S. Sugirtharajah, ed., *The Postcolonial Biblical Reader* (Malden, MA: Wiley-Blackwell, 2006).

of the story: Deborah develops the plan for entrapping the Canaanite forces and describes it to Barak, whose only response is to state unequivocally that he will not participate—will not lead armies to save Israel from the Canaanite oppressors—unless Deborah goes with him. While one could initially read this as Barak's appropriately honoring the prophetic vision of Deborah and wanting to consult her as events unfold, most of what we are told in the following narrative belies the intuition that Barak is courageous. Deborah explicitly refutes the suggestion that this battle—and by extension, this narrative—will lead to Barak's glory, for God will give the enemy commander into "the hand of a woman" (4:9). This is clearly projected to be an unexpected turn of events counterposed to a traditional understanding of masculine valor in war. Further, Deborah has to prompt and reassure Barak at the right moment for attack ("Up! For this is the day on which the LORD has given Sisera into your hand. The LORD is indeed going out before you"; 4:14). Male military potency has been thoroughly ironized even before the narrating of Jael's execution of Sisera.

The prose version then continues to unfold with significant dramatic irony: Jael invites Sisera to "have no fear," but of course he should have feared her. When he commands her to stand guard at the tent entrance, his caution regarding potential malefactors from outside is shown to be inadequate when in the next verse Jael steals over to him and kills him herself. The immediacy of that action is telling: Jael does not murmur assent to Sisera's command, nor does the narrative have her standing at the tent flap for some time until Sisera falls asleep. The rapid pacing highlights the foolishness and ignorance of the Canaanite commander: "'Guard me from [other] enemies!' And she killed him." The decisiveness of Jael echoes and amplifies the decisiveness of Deborah earlier in the narrative. Military strategy and valor are gendered in unexpected bodies here: female bodies, to the implicit shame of Sisera and the explicit shame of the Israelite military commander, Barak.

It is no simple thing, however, to claim the figure of Jael as one that supports women's agency specifically. One might argue that the narrator's construction of Jael entirely co-opts her character for the (normally male-gendered) military endeavor of Israelite holy war. We could argue that Jael's performance of a battle role simply renders her "masculinized" in a culture in which only males were warriors. Or one might press a reading of Jael as transgendered, for as Gale Yee notes, "In violating the traditional boundaries of her sex, the woman warrior is [an] anomaly. Neither male nor female, as these are customarily construed, she is a liminal figure."[19] But one could also

19. Gale A. Yee, "By the Hand of a Woman: The Metaphor of the Woman Warrior in Judges 4," *Semeia* 61 (1993): 99.

object, as Daniel I. Block does, that neither gender equity nor the subversion of patriarchal arrogance is the point of this story. One may still read resistantly on any number of levels, but these objections demonstrate the complicated and contestatory nature of interpreting gender in these texts.

> "While feminist approaches offer many fresh insights into the biblical text, too often modern agendas are imposed upon these ancient documents, overriding and obscuring the original intention of the narrator/song writer. In their enthusiasm to celebrate the subversion of patriarchy, such interpretations subvert the authority of God and obscure the message he seeks to communicate through this text. The biblical author was obviously interested in women's affairs and achievements, but in the final analysis Deborah and Jael are not heroic figures because of their revisionist challenges to prevailing social structures; they are heroines because of what they accomplish as agents of the divine agenda, which in this instance has less to do with overthrowing oppressive patriarchy than the role they play in Yahweh's overthrowing oppressive Canaanites."
> —Daniel I. Block, *Judges, Ruth* (2002), 186

The implicit suggestion of threatened sexual violence in this story begs for analysis as well. The practice of sexual violation of enemy women for the purpose of long-term destabilization of the enemy is a well-known and amply documented strategy of male warriors in many cultures, from ancient times to today. Scripture testifies to this abhorrent practice in holy-war texts such as Numbers 31:18, in which Moses commands the execution of nonvirgin Midianite women but allows his army to "keep alive for" themselves Midianite virgin girls, and Deuteronomy 20:14, which instructs that enemy women may be taken as booty. On the local level of ancient Israelite social practice, for a man to enter the tent of an unrelated woman who has no male chaperone present falls outside the norms of the patriarchal society of ancient Israel: to a significant degree, the honor of the Israelite family was predicated on the ability of male kinsmen to guard the sexual purity of the family's females. Many readers—and not only those who identify as feminists—have seen in the narrative of Jael's execution of Sisera a reversal of the threat of rape. Although Jael is unquestionably the vulnerable one when this warrior first approaches her tent, she ends up penetrating his body violently instead. Her penetration of him is a devastating ironic reversal of phallic power that simultaneously masculinizes Jael and feminizes Sisera according to holy war's phallocentric cultural script.

Finally, we may look through the lens of postcolonial criticism at the dynamics of power in this passage. Judges 4 establishes Israel as a subjugated people that rises up against a cruel imperial power. Already, though, we sense that this is a complicated kind of storytelling, for it is only because Israel disobeyed God's command to subjugate the Canaanites that Israel finds itself now in a position of powerlessness. The rapacious territorial aggression of Israel is authorized at the opening of the book of Judges: "The Lord said, 'Judah shall go up [to fight against the Canaanites]. I hereby give the land into his hand'" (1:2), and the conquest rhetoric unfolds from there. But Israel fails to dispossess and exterminate the Canaanites completely, so God chooses to sell them into the power of their enemies (2:14). Again we ask: Who is the conqueror here and who is the conquered? The Israelites' victimization has been thoroughly deconstructed even before we hear them groaning under the iron hand of Jabin.

We might reflect also on the colonization of Jael by the militaristic rhetoric of Judges 4–5. She is the indigenous female Other whose body would have been consumed by the invader—in this case Sisera, who breaches the boundary of her tent—had she not fought back. The prose and poetic versions alike make Jael into the ideal subaltern: she is a metonym for the enemy who mimics the violence of the empire against its own people in order to save itself, as Rahab had done before her (Josh. 2). Lori L. Rowlett's analysis of colonialist dynamics in the story of Rahab and the Disney movie *Pocahontas* may be applied to Jael as well:

> There are two ways to control living beings—eradication and domestication. Eradication means simply exterminating people; extermination abolishes power by abolishing its object. Domestication, as in the stories of Rahab and Pocahontas, represents an attempt to bring the populace into line, so that the colonized support the dominating culture without coercion. . . . Therefore it is essential that the colonizing culture represent the indigenous people as voluntarily complicit in their own domination.[20]

Indeed, the poetic version of our story is particularly insistent about valorizing those who "offer themselves willingly" (5:2, 9). In the chilling performance of power that is Judges 5, an invitation to submit is extended to the implied audience through the body of Jael. That invitation suggests that the indigenous "Canaanites"—real and metaphorical, external to Israel and within the community—submit to the rhetoric of colonization or die.

20. Lori L. Rowlett, "Disney's Pocahontas and Joshua's Rahab in Postcolonial Perspective," in *Culture, Entertainment and the Bible*, ed. George Aichele (Sheffield: Sheffield Academic Press, 2000), 72.

Thus Canaan colonizes Israel in a temporary narratological feint (lasting twenty years; 4:3) that actually serves to throw the ruthless power of the Israelites and their God into sharper relief. Israel, in fact, is the imperial power here, colonizing the Canaanite foils who stand as minor inconveniences in the Israelite holy-war narrative and colonizing the spiritual imaginations of those who are drawn into this battle through the pages of our Bibles. There is escape neither for Sisera nor for us. And so we must continue to wrestle with these holy and disturbing texts. I can only hope that our excursion into feminist, womanist, queer, and postcolonial hermeneutics has equipped you to begin to learn some new holds in this wrestling that we do with our beloved Scripture.

FOR FURTHER READING

Day, Linda, and Carolyn Pressler, eds. *Engaging the Bible in a Gendered World: An Introduction to Feminist Biblical Interpretation in Honor of Katharine Doob Sakenfeld.* Louisville, KY: Westminster John Knox Press, 2006.

Goss, Robert E., and Mona West, eds. *Take Back the Word: A Queer Reading of the Bible.* Cleveland: Pilgrim Press, 2000.

Kwok, Pui-lan. *Postcolonial Imagination and Feminist Theology.* Louisville, KY: Westminster John Knox Press, 2005.

Lapsley, Jacqueline E. *Whispering the Word: Hearing Women's Stories in the Old Testament.* Louisville, KY: Westminster John Knox Press, 2005.

Segovia, Fernando F. *Decolonizing Biblical Studies: A View from the Margins.* Maryknoll, NY: Orbis Books, 2000.

Sugirtharajah, R. S. *Postcolonial Criticism and Biblical Interpretation.* Oxford: Oxford University Press, 2002.

———, ed. *Voices from the Margin: Interpreting the Bible in the Third World.* Rev. and expanded 3rd ed. Maryknoll, NY: Orbis Books, 2006.

5

Wrestling the Word

Scripture beckons! The dramatic narratives and eloquent poems and brilliant aphorisms and passionate exhortations of Scripture invite us into a sustained attentiveness to the relationship between God and God's people. Scripture also invites us into a profound and tensive engagement with our own practices of interpretation. I hope that this book has helped you to think rigorously and deeply about your own hermeneutics wherever and whenever you engage Scripture, whether for the seminary classroom or for a parish Bible study, for sermon preparation or private devotional reading or research for a scholarly article.

COLLABORATIVE DIASPORA THEOLOGY

In a 2004 essay, I called for the creation of a multivocal Old Testament theology that was grounded in the metaphor of "exile" and responsive to the articulations of isolation, abandonment, and displacement that we hear in Scripture. I envisioned a collaborative work that would be attentive to the situated contexts of the contributors and the implied audience(s), a creative polyphony that would dare to argue "passionately against itself within its own pages so as to destabilize its own unanticipated rigidities and inadvertent claims to normativity."[1] Such collaboration would be theologically and sociopolitically attentive to the diasporas of marginalized persons across

1. Carolyn J. Sharp, "The Trope of 'Exile' and the Displacement of Old Testament Theology," *Perspectives in Religious Studies* 31 (2004): 153–69.

the globe as a significant "site"—literally and metaphorically—of biblical theologizing for those who follow an incarnate Lord.

In the biblical studies academy, opportunities are increasing for collaborative work across disciplinary lines. This is a heartening development that matters not only for theological schools but also for the church. What are some of the indicators of this movement toward more integrative and cross-disciplinary conversation? One sign is the increasing number of interdisciplinary groups within the Society of Biblical Literature. The African American Biblical Hermeneutics section claims as its mission "to engage in the interdisciplinary and holistic study of the Bible and its place in a multi-faceted and complex African-American cultural Weltanschauung."[2] The Bible and Cultural Studies section names their work as interdisciplinary and encourages "comparative analyses of the Bible as artefact and icon in word, image, and sound," going on to say that they "offer a forum for pursuing cultural analyses of gender, race, and class both within the social world of ancient Mediterranean cultures and in dialogue with modern cultural representations." The Gospel and Our Culture Network Forum on Missional Hermeneutics "draws together biblical scholars, theologians, graduate students, and ministry practitioners from a range of disciplines and ecclesiological contexts" to explore "the intersections of missiology, ecclesiology, and biblical scholarship in the interpretation of the Bible as it serves the missional vocation of the church."[3] The Reading, Theory, and the Bible section "provides a forum to encourage innovative and experimental approaches to biblical studies, to facilitate critical reflection on the role of theory in reading, and to support biblical scholarship informed by cross-disciplinary conversation." Other interdisciplinary groups could be named as well. These are exciting times for biblical studies!

Here is another sign of movement toward a collaborative ethos: an innovative new commentary series has been established that fosters joint work by North American and German partners on each biblical book. Appropriate to its fostering of intellectual partnership, the series itself has a dual name: the International Exegetical Commentary on the Old Testament (IECOT) / Internationaler exegetischer Kommentar zum Alten Testament (IEKAT). As the prospectus for the new series explains, "This series of commentaries is designed to be

- *international*: For the first time in the history of Bible commentaries, both a German and an English version are being edited simultaneously.

2. The Web site for the African American Biblical Hermeneutics Section is http://www.hrpj.com/aabhs.html.

3. The Web site for the Gospel and Our Culture Network is http://gocn.org.

- *ecumenical*: The group of editors and authors includes Protestant, Catholic, and Jewish biblical scholars.
- *contemporary*: The main feature of the commentary is the interlinkage of both synchronic and diachronic perspectives in analysis of texts. Other emphases include treatment of social-historical background, liberation-theological viewpoints, gender aspects and elements of the history of reception."

This series promises to be groundbreaking in its dialogic approach to the biblical texts themselves and to the production of scholarly literature about the texts.

Why are interdisciplinarity and collaboration important? First, the Hebrew Scriptures are richly complex and for all intents and purposes intercultural, given the wide variety of Israelite and Judean groups whose texts and traditions are represented over a period of centuries and given the influence on ancient Israelite literature of Canaanite, Egyptian, and other cultures and literatures. A variety of hermeneutical methods and interpretive paradigms should be deployed in order effectively to elucidate the many dimensions of these texts. Second, no one theory or interpretive posture should be allowed to pronounce in stentorian fashion on the elements of the texts that it finds most important. By its very nature, interdisciplinary collaborative work tends to decenter the epistemological assumptions of particular ways of knowing in favor of a fluid interchange among various languages and epistemologies. This is all to the good and will benefit, again, not only the academy but also the church.

Perhaps most important, interdisciplinarity and collaboration are vital because we learn from each other when we read in community. This is true whether "community" is construed as your biblical studies class, your Bible study group or clergy support group, your church, your denomination, or Christian tradition writ more broadly through the centuries. Can you see the great cloud of witnesses gathered around you as you read? Allow your imagination to wander freely through the halls of your theological school, among those gathered for worship in your church, out into the streets of your community, and on through the cathedrals of England and the monastic cells of Egypt, across the landscapes of North American and European and African and Asian biblical interpretation, and even through the mists of time separating you from countless medieval and patristic readers of Scripture. So many persuasive and disturbing and devout and misguided and wonderfully creative readings have been generated by the people of God! We can only benefit from listening to them all in the presence of God and one another. And we will be incalculably enriched by listening to the reasons, passionate and urgent, that have motivated believers to engage the Word in their prayer life, in their writing, and in their worship.

CONSTRUCTING AND RECONSTRUCTING YOUR OWN READING STRATEGIES

My students have shared with me some of their deep reasons for reading Scripture. It is a profound joy of the teaching vocation to hear what draws students to the Bible and to see their commitment despite the inevitable moments of interpretive frustration and occasional experiences of disjuncture between their lives and what Scripture says. Listen to their words below, which I supply as a way to evoke the rich diversity of hermeneutical desires in communities that listen for God's Word. These are student responses to a question I posed in class: "What kind of reader of Scripture do you want to become?"

> My pastor at home says that when you read the Scriptures enough or patiently enough, the Scriptures begin to read you. I think I like that. The basic and (perhaps) shallow answer is, I would like to become a "more faithful" reader. I bristle when difficult or even offensive texts are quickly explained away. The skills I want to develop are varied and diverse: elucidating sources and recognizing the realities surrounding the formation of the text are really important facets that then allow for an investigation of power present in that formation. The skill of listening for the rhetorical partners who do not speak in the text, or, when they do, speak as caricatures of themselves or their positions, is also one to build (while maybe stopping short of invention if possible!?). I would like to build more patience with the text, sitting with words and tropes that I receive in a certain way initially or don't understand at all. I would like to be attentive to the ways the text is unclear, recognizing that both authors and hearers of the text are (and have always been) in the process of navigating their particular understandings. (Bryce, a 27-year-old Presbyterian)

> I want to become the kind of reader who never stops being surprised by the biblical text and who never stops looking for different dimensions in the text. Learning Biblical Hebrew this year has begun (painfully slowly!) to help me with that, because everything is new, and everything sounds just a bit different in the Hebrew. I don't want to ever think that "I know" what the Bible says, or even to assume that about a smaller piece—what Isaiah says, for example. Everything I read in biblical interpretation, theology, and even in the newspaper can cause me to understand and approach reading differently. I guess it boils down to the fact that I want to become a reader who is continually aware of the dynamics of the text I am not seeing, but who is not preoccupied or distracted by that. (Liane, a 25-year-old Episcopalian)

> I hope to be a responsive reader of Scripture alert to what God is doing in my midst. I want to be led in my interactions with Scripture, and I want to be interactive. I want to marvel, ask questions, get frus-

trated, desire, and be moved by Scripture. I want to engage God and my community (some of whom follow Jesus, others who do not) with the soon-to-be contested "nuggets of truth" I might have received. I want to read Scripture for what it claims to be before weighing it down with other grids. If God's love is wide and long and high and deep, then I want to sit with that for a while. I want to imagine what that is like and even dare to feel it. I want my life and the lives of those around me to find relevance in Scripture not only through our struggle to be better readers of Scripture, but also because of God's faithfulness to find God's people anywhere—even in an ancient, confusing, wonderful book. (Joshua, a 24-year-old nondenominational churchgoer [Vineyard])

I have always had a dislike for certain breeds of literary criticism, the way these critics attempt to dismember the beauty and structure of dear and sacred text to make room in what cracks they have made to say something "new." I have no real answer as to why I have allowed what has been a lengthy and extensive education in poor reading techniques to read the Bible for me for so many years. I still believe that this is a beautiful and meaningful narrative. When I have been given eyes to see (by teachers, or the Spirit, I suppose), I have found the biblical narrative truer, more profoundly beautiful than any of the hundreds of others in which I tried to find meaning. I am always, always praying for eyes to see. (Ashleigh, a 23-year-old Anglican)

I was terribly ignorant of Old Testament Scripture. Growing up in a secular household, I read Scripture of a different kind. My sacred texts were by Jane Austen, Hemingway, Salinger, &c. Each day when I left the Old Testament Interpretation class, and at night reading the assigned texts, I was simply delighted and amazed. Challenged, yes, and troubled at times—but delighted. As for historical criticism, I think to see it as "flattening" is a failure of imagination. I was thrilled by the idea of these characters named J, E, D, and P, and (though I know they were not each one person but many people, schools of people) each had a personality all his or her own. For instance, I imagined P a bit like Rain Man—muttering to himself, obsessively writing lists, dates, weights and measures, and genealogies. (Lisa, a 32-year-old Roman Catholic)

I want to be able to read every word as if I were reading it for the first time, and I want to read it as if my life depended on it. (Ann, a 69-year-old member of the United Church of Christ)

Bryce wants to listen for voices that do not speak in the text or that have been rendered as unreliable. He is attentive to the power of Scripture for formation, and so he wants to build the capacity to listen patiently for ambiguities and ongoing negotiations within the text.

Liane cherishes hermeneutical surprises. She is courageous about learning a new diction, that of Biblical Hebrew. She wants to guard against the possibility of commodifying the witness of Scripture in her reading practices.

Joshua prizes the mutuality of robust engagement with a Word that leads him even as he is reading it. He wants to marvel at the truth of what he sees in the pages of Scripture, and he yearns to come up against the powerful reality of God's love as he reads.

Ashleigh resists hermeneutical practices that violate the integrity of the biblical text. She wants to see Scripture whole, honoring its beauty and reading with eyes wide open to its transformative power.

Lisa delights in the interpretive enterprise of listening for different textual voices. She declines any way of reading that will yield a text less dramatic and imaginative than she knows Scripture to be.

Ann longs for the freshness of hermeneutical innocence even as she realizes, with the wisdom of a seasoned exegete, that our lives just might depend on our encounters with the sacred in Scripture.

How do you read?

What kind of Scripture reader do *you* want to become?

The Hebrew Scriptures help us know God, and they help us know ourselves. These texts have an extraordinary capacity to help us "hear one another into speech," in the words of feminist theologian Nelle Morton.[4] Wrestling with these texts, we encounter a word that endures forever (Isa. 40:8), a word that is infinitely more powerful than we are and yet that offers itself to us willingly as gift, as challenge, as truth. Whenever we wrestle with Scripture—whether robustly or tentatively, whether joyfully or anxiously—we are doing precisely what Amos commanded the people of God to do: "Seek the Lord and live!" (5:6).

Yes, sometimes wrestling feels like struggle, and sometimes it feels like play. Some of the time, we walk away limping. But always remember this: as we wrestle together, vulnerable in community, we just might glimpse the face of God.

4. Nelle Morton (1905–1987) was an antiracism activist, educator, and feminist theologian. Prominent among her written works is *The Journey Is Home* (Boston: Beacon Press, 1985).

Bibliography

Ackroyd, Peter. *Exile and Restoration*. Philadelphia: Westminster Press, 1968.

Arnold, Bill T., and Bryan E. Beyer, eds. *Readings from the Ancient Near East: Primary Sources for Old Testament Study*. Grand Rapids: Baker Academic, 2002.

Auerbach, Erich. "Odysseus' Scar." In *Mimesis*, 3–23. Garden City, NY: Doubleday, 1953.

Baden, Joel S. *J, E, and the Redaction of the Pentateuch*. Forschungen zum Alten Testament 68. Tübingen: Mohr Siebeck, 2009.

Bakhtin, Mikhail M. *The Dialogic Imagination: Four Essays*. Edited by Michael Holquist. Translated by Caryl Emerson and Michael Holquist. Austin: University of Texas Press, 1981.

Barstad, Hans M. "History and the Hebrew Bible." In *Can a "History of Israel" Be Written?* edited by Lester L. Grabbe, 37–64. Journal for the Study of the Old Testament Supplement Series 245. European Seminar in Historical Methodology 1. Sheffield: Sheffield Academic Press, 1997.

Barton, John. *The Nature of Biblical Criticism*. Louisville, KY: Westminster John Knox Press, 2007.

———. *Reading the Old Testament: Method in Biblical Study*. Revised and enlarged. Louisville, KY: Westminster John Knox Press, 1996.

Batto, Bernard F. *Slaying the Dragon: Mythmaking in the Biblical Tradition*. Louisville, KY: Westminster/John Knox Press, 1992.

Bhabha, Homi K. *The Location of Culture*. London: Routledge, 1994. Repr., 2005.

Bible and Culture Collective, The. *The Postmodern Bible*. New Haven, CT: Yale University Press, 1995.

Blenkinsopp, Joseph. *The Pentateuch*. New York: Doubleday, 1992.

Block, Daniel I. *Judges, Ruth*. New American Commentary 6. Nashville: Broadman & Holman, 2002.

Boadt, Lawrence. *Reading the Old Testament: An Introduction*. New York: Paulist Press, 1984.

Boer, Roland, ed. *Bakhtin and Genre Theory in Biblical Studies*. Atlanta: Society of Biblical Literature, 2007.

Boling, Robert G. *Judges*. Anchor Bible 6A. New York: Doubleday, 1975.

Braziel, Jana Evans, and Anita Mannur, eds. *Theorizing Diaspora*. Oxford: Blackwell Pub., 2003.

Brenneman, James. *Canons in Conflict: Negotiating Texts in True and False Prophecy*. Oxford: Oxford University Press, 1997.

Brenner, Athalya. *I Am . . . : Biblical Women Tell Their Own Stories*. Minneapolis: Fortress Press, 2005.

———, ed. *Judges*. A Feminist Companion to the Bible, 2nd ser. Sheffield: Sheffield Academic Press, 1999.

Bright, John. *A History of Israel*. 4th ed. Louisville, KY: Westminster John Knox Press, 2000.

Brown, Michael Joseph. *Blackening of the Bible: The Aims of African American Biblical Scholarship*. New York: Trinity Press International, 2004.

Brown, William P. *Seeing the Psalms: A Theology of Metaphor*. Louisville, KY: Westminster John Knox Press, 2002.

Brueggemann, Walter. *David's Truth in Israel's Imagination and Memory*. Minneapolis: Fortress Press, 1985.

———. *Mandate to Difference: An Invitation to the Contemporary Church*. Louisville, KY: Westminster John Knox Press, 2007.

———. *The Prophetic Imagination*. 2nd ed. Minneapolis: Fortress Press, 2001.

———. "Psalms and the Life of Faith: A Suggested Typology of Function." In *The Psalms and the Life of Faith*, edited by Patrick D. Miller, 3–32. Minneapolis: Fortress Press, 1995.

———. *Texts under Negotiation: The Bible and Postmodern Imagination*. Minneapolis: Fortress Press, 1993.

———. "Theology of the Old Testament: A Prompt Retrospect." In *God in the Fray: A Tribute to Walter Brueggemann*, edited by Tod Linafelt and Timothy K. Beal, 307–20. Minneapolis: Fortress Press, 1998.

———. *Theology of the Old Testament: Testimony, Dispute, Advocacy*. Minneapolis: Fortress Press, 1997.

Cannon, Katie G., Alison P. Gise Johnson, and Angela D. Sims. "Womanist Works in Word." *Journal of Feminist Studies in Religion* 21 (2005): 135–46.

Carr, David M. *Reading the Fractures of Genesis: Historical and Literary Approaches*. Louisville, KY: Westminster John Knox Press, 1996.

———. "What Is Required to Identify Pre-Priestly Narrative Connections between Genesis and Exodus? Some General Reflections and Specific Cases." In *A Farewell to the Yahwist? The Composition of the Pentateuch in Recent European Interpretation*, edited by Thomas B. Dozeman and Konrad Schmid, 159–80. Leiden: E. J. Brill, 2006.

Carroll, Robert P. "Madonna of Silences: Clio and the Bible." In *Can a "History of Israel" Be Written?* edited by Lester L. Grabbe, 84–103. Journal for the Study of the Old Testament Supplement Series 245. European Seminar in Historical Methodology 1. Sheffield: Sheffield Academic Press, 1997.

Chavalas, Mark W., ed. *The Ancient Near East: Historical Sources in Translation*. Blackwell Sourcebooks in Ancient History. Oxford: Blackwell Pub., 2006.

Clines, David J. A. "Metacommentating Amos." In *Of Prophets' Visions and the Wisdom of Sages: Essays in Honour of R. Norman Whybray on His Seventieth Birthday*, edited by Heather A. McKay and David J. A. Clines, 142–60. Sheffield: JSOT Press, 1993.

———. "Response to Rolf Rendtorff," in "What Happened to the Yahwist? Reflections after Thirty Years: A Collegial Conversation between Rolf Rendtorff, David J. A. Clines, Allen Rosengren, and John Van Seters." In *Probing the Frontiers of Biblical Studies*, edited by J. Harold Ellens and John T. Greene, 39–66. Eugene, OR: Pickwick Pubs., 2009.

Collins, Adela Yarbro, and John J. Collins. *King and Messiah as Son of God: Divine, Human, and Angelic Messianic Figures in Biblical and Related Literature*. Grand Rapids: Wm. B. Eerdmans Pub. Co., 2008.

Collins, John J. *The Bible after Babel: Historical Criticism in a Postmodern Age*. Grand Rapids: Wm. B. Eerdmans Pub. Co., 2005.

———. *Does the Bible Justify Violence?* Minneapolis: Fortress Press, 2004.

———. *Introduction to the Hebrew Bible*. Minneapolis: Fortress Press, 2004.

Coogan, Michael D. *The Old Testament: A Historical and Literary Introduction to the Hebrew Scriptures*. Oxford: Oxford University Press, 2006.

Cooper-White, Pamela. *Shared Wisdom: Use of the Self in Pastoral Care and Counseling*. Minneapolis: Fortress Press, 2004.

Davies, Philip R. "Biblical Israel in the Ninth Century?" In *Understanding the History of Ancient Israel*, edited by H. G. M. Williamson, 49–56. New York: Oxford University Press, 2007.

———. *Memories of Ancient Israel: An Introduction to Biblical History—Ancient and Modern*. Louisville, KY: Westminster John Knox Press, 2008.

Davis, Ellen F. *Getting Involved with God: Rediscovering the Old Testament*. Cambridge, MA: Cowley Pubs., 2001.

Day, Linda, and Carolyn Pressler, eds. *Engaging the Bible in a Gendered World: An Introduction to Feminist Biblical Interpretation in Honor of Katharine Doob Sakenfeld*. Louisville, KY: Westminster John Knox Press, 2006.

Deleuze, Gilles. *The Logic of Sense*. Translated by Mark Lester with Charles Stivale. New York: Columbia University Press, 1990. Originally published as *Logique du sens*. Paris: Éditions de Minuit, 1969.

Dever, William G. *What Did the Biblical Writers Know and When Did They Know It? What Archaeology Can Tell Us about the Reality of Ancient Israel*. Grand Rapids: Wm. B. Eerdmans Pub. Co., 2001.

Dozeman, Thomas B. "The Commission of Moses and the Book of Genesis." In *A Farewell to the Yahwist? The Composition of the Pentateuch in Recent European Interpretation*, edited by Thomas B. Dozeman and Konrad Schmid, 107–29. Leiden: E. J. Brill; Boston: Society of Biblical Literature, 2006.

Eskenazi, Tamara Cohn. "Introduction—Facing the Text as Other: Some Implications of Lévinas's Work for Biblical Studies." In *Lévinas and Biblical Studies*, edited by Tamara Cohn Eskenazi, Gary A. Phillips, and David Jobling, 1–16. Atlanta: Society of Biblical Literature, 2003.

Finkelstein, Israel, and Amihai Mazar. *The Quest for the Historical Israel: Debating Archaeology and the History of Early Israel*. Leiden: E. J. Brill, 2007.

Fretheim, Terence E. *The Pentateuch*. Interpreting Biblical Texts. Nashville: Abingdon Press, 1996.

———. "Some Reflections on Brueggemann's God." In *God in the Fray: A Tribute to Walter Brueggemann*, edited by Tod Linafelt and Timothy K. Beal, 24–37. Minneapolis: Fortress Press, 1998.

Fuchs, Esther. "Biblical Feminisms: Knowledge, Theory and Politics in the Study of Women in the Hebrew Bible." *Biblical Interpretation* 16 (2008): 205–26.

Gafney, Wilda C. "A Black Feminist Approach to Biblical Studies." *Encounter* 67 (2006): 391–403.

———. *Daughters of Miriam: Women Prophets in Ancient Israel*. Minneapolis: Fortress Press, 2008.

Geniesse, Jane Fletcher. *Passionate Nomad: The Life of Freya Stark*. New York: Modern Library, 2001.

Gillingham, Susan E. *One Bible, Many Voices: Different Approaches to Biblical Studies*. Grand Rapids: Wm. B. Eerdmans Pub. Co., 1998.

Gnuse, Robert K. "Redefining the Elohist?" *Journal of Biblical Literature* 119 (2000): 201–20.

Goss, Robert E., and Mona West, eds. *Take Back the Word: A Queer Reading of the Bible.* Cleveland: Pilgrim Press, 2000.

Grabbe, Lester L. *Ancient Israel: What Do We Know and How Do We Know It?* New York: T&T Clark, 2007.

Green, Barbara. *Mikhail Bakhtin and Biblical Scholarship: An Introduction.* Atlanta: Society of Biblical Literature, 2000.

Guest, Deryn. "Looking Lesbian at the Bathing Bathsheba." *Biblical Interpretation* 16 (2008): 227–62.

Guest, Deryn, Robert E. Goss, Mona West, and Thomas Bohache, eds. *Queer Bible Commentary*. London: SCM Press, 2006.

Gunn, David M. *Judges*. Blackwell Bible Commentaries. Oxford: Blackwell Pub., 2005.

Halpern, Baruch. *David's Secret Demons: Messiah, Murderer, Traitor, King*. Grand Rapids: Wm. B. Eerdmans Pub. Co., 2001.

Harries, Karsten. "Metaphor and Transcendence." In *On Metaphor*, edited by Sheldon Sacks, 71–88. Chicago: University of Chicago Press, 1979.

Hayes, John H., and Carl R. Holladay. *Biblical Exegesis: A Beginner's Handbook*. 3rd ed. Louisville, KY: Westminster John Knox Press, 2007.

Hess, Richard S. *Israelite Religions: An Archaeological and Biblical Survey*. Grand Rapids: Baker Academic, 2007.

Hoffmeier, James K. *Israel in Egypt: The Evidence for the Authenticity of the Exodus Tradition*. New York: Oxford University Press, 1997.

Keefe, Alice A. *Woman's Body and the Social Body in Hosea*. Journal for the Study of the Old Testament Supplement Series 338. Gender, Culture, Theory 10. Sheffield: Sheffield Academic Press, 2001.

Keirsey, David. *Please Understand Me II: Temperament, Character, Intelligence*. Del Mar, CA: Prometheus Nemesis, 1998.

———, and Marilyn Bates. *Please Understand Me: Character and Temperament Types*. Del Mar, CA: Prometheus Nemesis, 1984.

Kim, Uriah Y. "Postcolonial Criticism: Who Is the Other in the Book of Judges?" In *Judges and Method: New Approaches in Biblical Studies*, edited by Gale A. Yee, 161–82. 2nd ed. Minneapolis: Fortress Press, 2007.

Kitchen, K. A. *On the Reliability of the Old Testament*. Grand Rapids: Wm. B. Eerdmans Pub. Co., 2003.

Klein, William W., Craig L. Blomberg, and Robert L. Hubbard Jr. *Introduction to Biblical Interpretation*. Dallas: Word, 1993.

Knohl, Israel. *The Divine Symphony: The Bible's Many Voices*. Philadelphia: Jewish Publication Society, 2003.

Kristeva, Julia. *Revolt, She Said: An Interview by Philippe Petit*. Translated by Brian O'Keeffe. Semiotext(e) Foreign Agents Series. Los Angeles: Semiotext(e), 2002.

———. *Strangers to Ourselves*. Translated by Leon S. Roudiez. New York: Columbia University Press, 1991.

Kwok, Pui-lan. *Postcolonial Imagination and Feminist Theology*. Louisville, KY: Westminster John Knox Press, 2005.

Lapsley, Jacqueline E. *Whispering the Word: Hearing Women's Stories in the Old Testament*. Louisville, KY: Westminster John Knox Press, 2005.

Levenson, Jon D. *The Hebrew Bible, the Old Testament, and Historical Criticism*. Louisville, KY: Westminster/John Knox Press, 1993.

Lévinas, Emmanuel. *Alterity and Transcendence*. Translated by Michael B. Smith. New York: Columbia University Press, 1999.

———. *Difficult Freedom: Essays on Judaism*. Translated by Seán Hand. London: Athlone Press, 1990.

Lipka, Hilary B. *Sexual Transgression in the Hebrew Bible*. Hebrew Bible Monographs 7. Sheffield: Sheffield Phoenix, 2006.

Maier, Christl M. *Daughter Zion, Mother Zion: Gender, Space, and the Sacred in Ancient Israel*. Minneapolis: Fortress Press, 2008.

Mandolfo, Carleen. *Daughter Zion Talks Back to the Prophets: A Dialogic Theology of the Book of Lamentations*. Semeia Studies 58. Atlanta: Society of Biblical Literature; Leiden: E. J. Brill, 2007.

———. *God in the Dock: Dialogic Tension in the Psalms of Lament*. Journal for the Study of the Old Testament Supplement Series 357. Sheffield: Sheffield Academic Press, 2003.

Martin, Wallace. "Metaphor." In *The New Princeton Handbook of Poetic Terms*, edited by T. V. F. Brogan, 184–90. Princeton, NJ: Princeton University Press, 1994.

Mayfield, Tyler. "The Accounts of Deborah (Judges 4–5) in Recent Research." *Currents in Biblical Research* 7 (2009): 306–35.

Mazar, Amihai. "The Spade and the Text: The Interaction between Archaeology and Israelite History Relating to the Tenth–Ninth Centuries BCE." In *Understanding the History of Ancient Israel*, edited by H. G. M. Williamson, 143–71. New York: Oxford, 2007.

McCann, J. Clinton. *Judges*. Interpretation. Louisville, KY: John Knox Press, 2002.

McKenzie, Steven L., and Stephen R. Haynes, eds. *To Each Its Own Meaning: An Introduction to Biblical Criticisms and Their Applications*. Rev. and expanded. Louisville, KY: Westminster John Knox Press, 1999.

Miller, J. Maxwell, and John H. Hayes. *A History of Ancient Israel and Judah*. 2nd ed. Louisville, KY: Westminster John Knox Press, 2006.

Monroe, Irene. "When and Where I Enter, Then the Whole Race Enters with Me: Que(e)rying Exodus." In *Take Back the Word: A Queer Reading of the Bible*, edited by Robert E. Goss and Mona West, 82–91. Cleveland: Pilgrim Press, 2000.

Morley, Neville. *Theories, Models and Concepts in Ancient History*. Approaching the Ancient World. London: Routledge, 2004.

Morton, Nelle. *The Journey Is Home*. Boston: Beacon Press, 1985.

Natoli, Joseph, and Linda Hutcheon, eds. *A Postmodern Reader*. Albany: State University of New York Press, 1993.

Newsom, Carol A. "Bakhtin, the Bible, and Dialogic Truth." *Journal of Religion* 76 (1996): 290–306.

———. *The Book of Job: A Contest of Moral Imaginations*. Oxford: Oxford University Press, 2003.

Nicholson, Ernest. *The Pentateuch in the Twentieth Century: The Legacy of Julius Wellhausen*. Oxford: Clarendon Press, 1998.

Niditch, Susan. *Judges*. Old Testament Library. Louisville, KY: Westminster John Knox Press, 2008.

Njoroge, Nyambura J. "The Bible and African Christianity: A Curse or a Blessing?" In *Other Ways of Reading: African Women and the Bible*, edited by Musa W. Dube, 207–36. Atlanta: Society of Biblical Literature; Geneva: WCC Publications, 2001.

Noth, Martin. *A History of Pentateuch Traditions*. Translated by Bernhard W. Anderson. Atlanta: Scholars Press, 1981.

Oldenburg, Ulf. *The Conflict between El and Ba'al in Canaanite Religion*. Leiden: E. J. Brill, 1969.

Olivier, Bert. "Nature as 'Abject,' Critical Psychology, and 'Revolt': The Pertinence of Kristeva." *South African Journal of Psychology* 37 (2007): 443–69.

Provan, Iain, V. Philips Long, and Tremper Longman III. *A Biblical History of Israel*. Louisville, KY: Westminster John Knox Press, 2003.

Punt, Jeremy. "Queer Theory Intersecting with Postcolonial Theory in Biblical Interpretation." *Council of Societies for the Study of Religion Bulletin* 35 (2006): 30–34.

Rad, Gerhard von. *Genesis*. Old Testament Library. Philadelphia: Westminster Press, 1972.

Rendtorff, Rolf. "The Paradigm Is Changing—Hopes and Fears." In *Israel's Past in Present Research: Essays on Ancient Israelite Historiography*, edited by V. Philips Long, 51–68. Winona Lake, IN: Eisenbrauns, 1999.

———. *The Problem of the Process of Transmission in the Pentateuch*. Journal for the Study of the Old Testament Supplement Series 89. Sheffield: Sheffield Academic Press, 1990. Translation of *Das überlieferungsgeschichtliche Problem das Pentateuch*. Beihefte zur alttestamentliche Wissenschaft 147. Berlin: de Gruyter, 1977.

Riso, Don Richard, and Russ Hudson. *The Wisdom of the Enneagram: The Complete Guide to Psychological and Spiritual Growth for the Nine Personality Types*. New York: Bantam Books, 1999.

Rohr, Richard, and Andreas Ebert. *The Enneagram: A Christian Perspective*. Translated by Peter Heinegg. New York: Crossroad, 2009. Originally published as *Das Enneagram: Die 9 Gesichter der Seele*. Munich: Claudius Verlag, 1989.

Rowlett, Lori L. "Disney's Pocahontas and Joshua's Rahab in Postcolonial Perspective." In *Culture, Entertainment and the Bible*, edited by George Aichele, 66–75. Journal for the Study of the Old Testament Supplement Series 309. Sheffield: Sheffield Academic Press, 2000.

Sanders, James A. *From Sacred Story to Sacred Text: Canon as Paradigm*. Philadelphia: Fortress Press, 1987.

Segovia, Fernando F. *Decolonizing Biblical Studies: A View from the Margins*. Maryknoll, NY: Orbis Books, 2000.

Sharp, Carolyn J. "The Formation of Godly Community: Old Testament Hermeneutics in the Presence of the Other." *Anglican Theological Review* 86 (2004): 623–36.

———. *Irony and Meaning in the Hebrew Bible*. Bloomington: Indiana University Press, 2009.

———. "The Trope of 'Exile' and the Displacement of Old Testament Theology." *Perspectives in Religious Studies* 31 (2004): 153–69.

Sherwood, Yvonne. *A Biblical Text and Its Afterlives: The Survival of Jonah in Western Culture*. Cambridge: Cambridge University Press, 2000.

———. *The Prostitute and the Prophet: Hosea's Marriage in Literary-Theoretical Perspective*. Journal for the Study of the Old Testament Supplement Series 212. Gender, Culture, Theory 2. Sheffield: Sheffield Academic Press, 1996.

Shiff, Richard. "Art and Life: A Metaphoric Relationship." In *On Metaphor*, edited by Sheldon Sacks, 105–20. Chicago: University of Chicago Press, 1979.

Smith, Mark S. *The Memoirs of God: History, Memory, and the Experience of the Divine in Ancient Israel*. Minneapolis: Fortress Press, 2004.

———. *Untold Stories: The Bible and Ugaritic Studies in the Twentieth Century*. Peabody, MA: Hendrickson Publishers, 2001.

Sommer, Benjamin D. *A Prophet Reads Scripture: Allusion in Isaiah 40–66*. Stanford, CA: Stanford University Press, 1998.

Spivak, Gayatri Chakravorty. *A Critique of Postcolonial Reason: Toward a History of the Vanishing Present*. Cambridge: Harvard University Press, 1999.

Sternberg, Meir. *The Poetics of Biblical Narrative: Ideological Literature and the Drama of Reading*. Bloomington: Indiana University Press, 1985.

Stone, Ken. "Lovers and Raisin Cakes: Food, Sex, and Divine Insecurity in Hosea." In *Queer Commentary and the Hebrew Bible*, edited by Ken Stone, 116–39. Cleveland: Pilgrim Press, 2001.

———. *Sex, Honor and Power in the Deuteronomistic History*. Journal for the Study of the Old Testament Supplement Series 234. Sheffield: Sheffield Academic Press, 1996.

———, ed. *Queer Commentary and the Hebrew Bible*. Cleveland: Pilgrim Press, 2001.

Sugirtharajah, R. S. *Postcolonial Criticism and Biblical Interpretation*. Oxford: Oxford University Press, 2002.

———, ed. *Still at the Margins: Biblical Scholarship Fifteen Years after the Voices from the Margin*. New York: T&T Clark, 2008.

———, ed. *Voices from the Margin: Interpreting the Bible in the Third World*. Rev. and expanded 3rd ed. Maryknoll, NY: Orbis Books, 2006.

Sullivan, Nikki. *A Critical Introduction to Queer Theory*. New York: New York University Press, 2003.

Thompson, Thomas L. *The Mythic Past: Biblical Archaeology and the Myth of Israel*. New York: Basic Books, 1999.

Trible, Phyllis. *God and the Rhetoric of Sexuality*. Overtures to Biblical Theology. Minneapolis: Fortress Press, 1978.

———. *Texts of Terror: Literary-Feminist Readings of Biblical Narratives*. Overtures to Biblical Theology. Minneapolis: Fortress Press, 1984.

van Wijk-Bos, Johanna W. H. *Making Wise the Simple: The Torah in Christian Faith and Practice*. Grand Rapids: Wm. B. Eerdmans Pub. Co., 2005.

Voelz, James W. "Multiple Signs, Levels of Meaning and Self as Text: Elements of Intertextuality." *Semeia* 69–70 (1995): 149–64.

Weems, Renita J. *Battered Love: Marriage, Sex, and Violence in the Hebrew Prophets*. Minneapolis: Fortress Press, 1995.

Westermann, Claus. *Genesis 37–50*. Continental Commentaries. Translated by John J. Scullion. Minneapolis: Augsburg Pub. House, 1986.

Whitelam, Keith W. "Setting the Scene: A Response to John Rogerson." In *Understanding the History of Ancient Israel*, edited by H. G. M. Williamson, 15–23. Proceedings of the British Academy 143. Oxford: Oxford University Press, 2007.

Whybray, R. N. *The Making of the Pentateuch: A Methodological Study*. Journal for the Study of the Old Testament Supplement Series 53. Sheffield: JSOT Press, 1987.

Wiegman, Robyn, ed. *Women's Studies on Its Own: A Next Wave Reader for Institutional Change*. Durham, NC: Duke University Press, 2002.

Wimbush, Vincent L., ed. *African Americans and the Bible: Sacred Texts and Social Textures*. With the assistance of Rosamond C. Rodman. New York: Continuum, 2003.

Yee, Gale A., ed. *Judges and Method: New Approaches in Biblical Studies*. 2nd ed. Minneapolis: Fortress Press, 2007.

———. *Poor Banished Children of Eve: Woman as Evil in the Hebrew Bible*. Minneapolis: Fortress Press, 2003.

Younger, K. Lawson, Jr. "Early Israel in Recent Biblical Scholarship." In *The Face of Old Testament Studies: A Survey of Contemporary Approaches*, edited by David W. Baker and Bill T. Arnold, 176–206. Grand Rapids: Baker Academic, 1999.

Scripture Index

HEBREW SCRIPTURES

Genesis
1 67
3:19 127
6–9 55
6:19 47
7:2 47
7:17 48
7:24 48
12–36 57
12:1–3 23
15:12–17 53
16 40
17:12–13 115
20:7 53
20:11 19
21 18n10, 40
22 23, 40
22:13 87
28:10–17 53
32:22–32 xiv
32:26–28 128
37 56
37–50 56–57
37:3a 56
37:4 56
37:5a 56
37:5–11 53
37:6–21 56
37:25–27 56
37:28a 56
38–39 56
40–41 56
40:1–41:36 53
41:34a 56
41:35b 56
41:41–45a 56
46 56
47–50 56

Exodus
3:14 48
14:12 128
18:8 54
32 39
33:7–11 52n3

Leviticus
19:2 61, 127

Numbers
13–14 55
20:14–21 54
25 35
31:18 131
32 55

Deuteronomy
6:5 128
20:14 131
20:16–18 42, 98
23:3–4 35

Joshua
2 132
6:25 35
7:11–12 128
11 105

Judges
1 41–42
1:2 132
1:19 105
2 41
2:11–22 74
2:14 132
4 xvi, 71–74, 132
4–5 36, 37, 71, 74–75, 104n22, 105, 132
4:2 74
4:3 41, 133
4:7 74
4:9 74, 130
4:14 74, 130
4:21 74
4:24 74

Judges (*continued*)
5 xvi, 71–74, 132
5:2 73, 132
5:7 73
5:9 73, 132
5:10 73
5:16–17 75
5:28 105

Ruth
4:13–22 35

1 Samuel
2:1–10 65
8 101n18
15:6 42

1 Chronicles
25:5–8 118

2 Chronicles
20 83

Nehemiah
6:14 118

Esther
9:5–14 83

Job
16:11–12 128
38–41 84

Psalms
8 67
19 66
22 71
22:23 128
44 66
62 66
68 74
74 66
88 66
97:4 89
146–150 66

Proverbs
7 37
7:23 37
8 119

Ecclesiastes
1:2 128

Isaiah
2:1–5 67
8:3 118
30:1–7 40
31:1–3 40
40:8 140
44 67
45:14 116
49:23 116
55:1–5 102

Jeremiah
46:1–24 40

Ezekiel
29:1–16 40

Hosea
11 67

Amos
1–2 70
4:13 70
5:6 140
5:8–9 70
9:5–6 70

Micah
4:1–4 67
6:6–8 128

NEW TESTAMENT

Matthew
5:5 89
16:24–25 89
23:11–12 89

Mark
8:34–35 89

Luke
9:23–24 89

Romans
11 98
13 32
13:13–14 32

Subject Index

Abraham (Abram), 19, 23–24, 53, 57, 62, 67, 92, 95, 98, 118, 127
Achan, 39
Adam, 62
African American hermeneutics, xiii, 122–23, 136, 136n2
African hermeneutics, 123–24
Ai, 93
Amnon, 117
Amorites, 41, 96
Amos
  book of, 1, 19, 29, 70
  the prophet, 22, 140
Anat, 36, 36n24
'apiru, 96
archaeology, 7, 17, 79, 92, 94–95, 103
Ashdod, 1
Asher, 74
Ashkelon, 1
Assyria, 40, 126
Augustine of Hippo, 24, 32–33
authorial intention, 3–6, 15, 43

Baal, 84, 89
Babylon, 40, 82, 126–27
Bakhtin, Mikhail, xiii, 63, 68–71, 74
Balaam, 53
Barak, 37, 72–74, 130
Bathsheba, 23, 101, 125
Bethel, 53
Bhabha, Homi, 126, 126n16
Brueggemann, Walter, xiii, 63–69, 72–73, 102–3
Butler, Judith, 124, 124n12

Carroll, Robert P., 120
Caton-Thompson, Gertrude, 79
Christ. *See* Jesus
clinical pastoral education (C.P.E.), 112
Cone, James, 113
Crusades, 97
Cyrus, 82

D. *See* Deuteronomist
Dahood, Mitchell, 87
Dan, 41, 74–75
Daniel, book of, 70, 127
David (king), 23, 35, 64, 75, 84, 94, 100–104, 116–17
Deborah, 37, 72–73, 118, 130–31
deconstruction, 35, 52, 120
Deuteronomist (D), 5, 33, 37, 41, 46–49, 55, 59–63, 70–72, 74–75, 139
  Deuteronomistic History, 109, 126
Deuteronomy, 45, 50, 110–11
Divine Warrior, 73–74, 89

Documentary Hypothesis, xiii, 45–47, 49–54, 58–59, 62–63, 71, 116

E. *See* Elohist
Ecclesiastes, 3, 23, 66
Egypt, 40, 56, 73, 84, 90–91, 94, 97–99, 128, 137
Ekron, 1
Elijah, 67
Elohim, 46, 48
Elohist (E), 46–50, 52, 52n3, 53–58, 60, 62, 71, 139
Emar, 118
Enneagram, 11, 11n7
Esther
  book of, 127
  as woman warrior, 36
Eve, 62
exodus, xi, 40–41, 58, 83, 90–92, 94–95, 97–100, 113, 118, 127
Exodus, book of, 40, 45, 48, 58, 90
Ezekiel, book of, 67, 118, 127
Ezra-Nehemiah, 127

feminist interpretation, xiii, 15, 18n10, 40, 113, 116–17, 119–23, 125, 129, 131, 133
Foucault, Michel, 124, 124n12

Gadites, 55
Garden of Eden, 29, 127
Gath, 1
Gaza, 1
Genesis, 19, 45, 48, 53, 57–58, 85
Gilead, 55, 74, 118
Girgashites, 96
Golden Calf, 39
Goliath, 103
Gutiérrez, Gustavo, 113

Hagar, 40, 115, 117–18
Hannah, 65
Hazor, 41, 93, 105
Heber, 42, 105
Heman, daughters of, 118
heteroglossia, 68
historical criticism, 6–7, 16–17, 20–22, 36, 64, 67, 104, 139
  historicity of biblical traditions, xiii, 80–81, 83, 90, 100, 102, 104, 106
historiography, 19, 94
  biblical, 12, 33, 83
    maximalist, 91–95
    minimalist, 91–95
Hittites, 96
holy war, 35n23, 36, 39, 41–43, 72–75, 95, 110, 130–33
Horeb, 48, 52–53
Hosea
  book of, 125
  the prophet, 125
Huldah, 118
Hurrians, 96
Hyksos, 90

interdisciplinary work, 9, 136–37
irony, 2–3, 14, 20, 22–23, 27–29, 51, 71, 71n25, 101, 130
Isaac, 23–24, 40, 95, 98
Isaiah, book of, 22, 116, 118, 138
Ishmaelites, 56

J. *See* Yahwist
Jabin, 41–42, 72–74, 105–6, 132
Jacob, xiv, 53, 56–57, 92, 95, 98, 111, 128
Jael, xvi, 36–37, 40–43, 71–74, 104–5, 129–32
Jebusites, 96
Jephthah's daughter, 117–18
Jeremiah
  book of, 13, 14, 127
  the prophet, 13
Jericho, 93, 115
Jerusalem, 70, 103, 119
Jesus (Christ), 29, 32–33, 40, 45–46, 71, 75, 77–79, 79n1, 88, 101, 118, 123–24, 139
Job
  book of, 66, 70
  sufferer, 23, 39, 70, 128
Joel, book of, 118
John, Gospel of, 29

Jonah
book of, 12, 51
the prophet, 12, 23, 83
Jonathan, 23, 116
Joseph, 23, 39, 53, 56–57
Joshua, book of, 35, 43, 45, 50, 90–91, 93, 96, 110
Judah (tribe), 132
Judges, book of, 23, 43, 71, 74, 90, 96, 101, 104–5, 117, 119n6, 132
Judith, 36

Kenites, 105
Kings, book of, 5, 50
kingship, 67, 79n1
Kishon, 73
Kristeva, Julia, xiii, 31–32, 32n20, 33–36, 71

Lamentations, 70
Leviathan, 84
Lévinas, Emmanuel, xiii, 31, 37, 37n25, 38–40, 42
Levite's concubine, 117–18
Leviticus, 45, 61
liberation theology, 113, 114n3
Luke, Gospel of, 111

Mari, 118
Mark, Gospel of, 29
Meroz, 75
Mesopotamia, 84
metaphor, xiv, 2, 5, 10, 14, 16, 22–23, 25–28, 32, 34, 40, 62, 65, 67–69, 75, 78, 88, 91, 98, 100, 115, 119–20, 135
Midianite(s), 56, 131
Miriam, 118
Moses, 42, 48, 55–56, 58–59, 67, 84, 90, 95, 98, 128, 131
Myers-Briggs Type Indicator, 11, 11n7

Naomi, 116
Naphtali, 72
Nebuchadnezzar, 82
Nineveh, 118
No'adiah, 118
Noth, Martin, 56
Numbers, 45, 50, 53

Oldenburg, Ulf, 85

P. *See* Priestly Writer
pastoral care, 20, 47, 63, 112, 112n1
Persia, 126–27
Philistines, 102, 105
Pocahontas, 132
postcolonial criticism, xiii, 109, 113, 126, 126n16, 127–29, 132–33
postcolonialism. *See* postcolonial criticism
postmodernism, 6–10, 14–16, 16n9, 17, 30–31, 49, 64, 67, 122, 127
Priestly Writer (P), 46–49, 54–63, 71, 75, 139
Psalms, book of, xv, 39, 66–67, 70, 84, 87, 89, 102, 115

Qohelet, 3, 39, 70
queer interpretation, xiii, 113, 124, 124n12, 125, 129, 133

Rahab, 35, 35n23, 42, 115, 132
Ras Shamra, 84
Rashi, 71
Red Sea, 73, 94
Reuben(ites), 55–56, 74–75
Ruether, Rosemary Radford, 113
Ruth, xvi, 22, 100, 115–16

Samson, 22–23, 100–101, 101n18
Sarah, xvi, 19, 23, 100, 118
Sargon, 84, 84n6
Saul, 23, 39, 75, 102
Segovia, Fernando F., 126
Seir, 73
Shasu, 96
Simeon, 56
Sinai, 48, 52–53, 84, 94, 98, 127
Sisera, xvi, 36–37, 40–43, 71–74, 104–5, 129–33
Sisera's mother, 72–74
Society of Biblical Literature, 92, 120, 136
Solomon(ic), 94, 103

source criticism. *See* Documentary Hypothesis
Spivak, Gayatri, 126, 126n16
Sugirtharajah, R. S., 129

Tamar, 117–18
Tel Dan inscription, 102
Ten Commandments, 84, 89
textual indeterminacy, 16, 29–30, 43
Trible, Phyllis, 117–18

Ugarit, 84
Ur, 23, 87

womanist interpretation, 113, 116–18, 120–23, 129, 133
women's studies, 122, 122n10

Yahwist (J), 46–50, 52, 54, 56–58, 60, 62, 71, 88, 139
Yehud, 126

Zebulun, 72
Zion, 70, 116, 119